THE SUSSEX BORDER PATH
Day Walks and Circular Routes

John Allen

Published by Sigma Leisure – an imprint of
Sigma Press, 1 South Oak Lane, Wilmslow, Cheshire SK9 6AR, England.

British Library Cataloguing in Publication Data
A CIP record for this book is available from the British Library.

ISBN: 1-85058-677-2

Typesetting and Design by: Sigma Press, Wilmslow, Cheshire.

Cover photograph: The Sussex Border Path, near Ditchling *(John Lloyd)*
Photography: The author
Maps: Michael Gilbert

Printed by: MFP Design and Print

Disclaimer: the information in this book is given in good faith and is believed to be correct at the time of publication. No responsibility is accepted by either the author or publisher for errors or omissions, or for any loss or injury howsoever caused. Only you can judge your own fitness, competence and experience.

Foreword

We are delighted to welcome this new guide to the Sussex Border Path as the 'official' definitive description of the route, superseding the previous Map Pack guide. It should prove to be a reliable companion whether you are walking the entire route or selecting from the series of excellent new circuits devised by John Allen.

There are now a large number of route descriptions for long distance paths. Having walked a great many, based on assorted themes, we would contend that the Sussex Border Path has more to offer than most. It invites you to explore some surprisingly remote corners of an increasingly crowded region of England (and likely to become more so as local planners are obliged to meet government housing quotas). The terrain, across the gently undulating farmed landscape of the Weald and over soft sandstone hills, is in marked contrast to the well known National Trails along the chalk ridges of the North and South Downs, which provide many walkers with their first taste of the landscape of South East England.

You may well ask, "Why try to follow what is only a boundary line on a map?" We have certainly not sought to follow the County boundary slavishly. In many places the route deviates substantially from the border in search of the best paths and to ensure minimal road walking. Nonetheless, the observant will note many natural and man-made features that determine the location of the County boundary, from earthen banks and the diverted River Mole skirting Gatwick Airport in West Sussex to the Kent Ditch in East Sussex.

When we devised the route, back in 1982, it was largely uncharted territory with few paths marked and many obstructed. Publication of our first guide drew attention to the problems, most of which have been resolved over the years. To celebrate their centenary, West Sussex County Council signposted the route in West Sussex in 1989. This was followed by waymarking in East Sussex, with the help of the Ramblers' Association, and Border Path signs are beginning to appear in Surrey and Kent. Mapping by the Ordnance Survey in the Landranger and Explorer series has further eased the potential navigator's problems. This new guide further complements these aids and will help to unravel the complexities of the route in some places. But don't be lulled into complacency, you may well still need to take and use a map and compass!

Aeneas Mackintosh and Ben Perkins

Dedication

This book is dedicated to Aeneas Mackintosh and Ben Perkins, who created the Sussex Border Path.

Preface

"A reeling road, a rolling road, that rambles round the shire"
G.K. Chesterton: The Rolling English Road

This book describes one of the best long-distance walks in England – the Sussex Border Path. It runs through 160 miles of unspoilt countryside, with constantly changing views, charming villages and small, friendly pubs. There are many fine old buildings, including Saxon and Norman churches, half-timbered houses large and small, and countless converted oasts. Ponds, first created for the iron industry, enhance many views.

This guide enables the Path to be tackled either as a series of one-day walks or as a continuous expedition. There are 26 self-contained walks, each with a description of the route, an alternative return, a sketch map and details of pubs, cafés, shops and places of interest.

Information about maps, accommodation, camping, travel, useful addresses and telephone numbers and books is also included.

Acknowledgements

It would be very remiss of me not to take the first opportunity to pay tribute to Aeneas Mackintosh and Ben Perkins, who created the Sussex Border Path and produced the first guide. It is one of those excellent ideas that is so obvious – once someone has had it. I am also grateful to them for writing the foreword. Thanks are also due to all those who have worked to remove obstructions and make the Path easier to follow.

I should also like to thank all those in Tourist Information Centres and the five County Councils who gave willing help with my enquiries. David Munn of East Sussex County Council was particularly helpful over rights of way. I am also indebted to Mrs Mavis Priestley and Mr Les O'Shea who checked the final manuscript and made many valuable suggestions.

John Allen

Contents

The Sussex Border Path

West Sussex

East Sussex

The Mid-Sussex Link

The Sussex Border Path

The Path runs from Thorney Island in West Sussex to Rye in East Sussex, sometimes straying into the neighbouring counties of Hampshire, Surrey and Kent. The Mid-Sussex Link follows the border between East and West Sussex from East Grinstead to Mile Oak, near Hove. The Path is described clockwise from west to east. The Mid-Sussex Link is described from north to south.

Ordnance Survey maps

Readers are strongly recommended to use OS maps in conjunction with this guide.

Landranger 1:50,000 (seven maps)

186 Aldershot & Guildford

187 Dorking, Reigate & Crawley

188 Maidstone & The Weald of Kent

189 Ashford & Romney Marsh

197 Chichester & The Downs

198 Brighton & Lewes

199 Eastbourne & Hastings

Explorer 1:25,000 (nine maps)

120 Chichester, South Harting & Selsey

122 (17) South Downs Way – Steyning to Newhaven

125 Romney Marsh, Rye & Winchelsea

133 Haslemere & Petersfield

134 Crawley & Horsham

135 (18) Ashdown Forest

136 The Weald, Royal Tonbridge Wells

146 Dorking, Boxhill and Reigate

147 Sevenoaks & Tonbridge

A number in brackets shows that the map has been renumbered, e.g. 122 was formerly 17.

The Explorer maps provide more detail and show the entire SBP. The Landranger maps cost less.

OS maps are not always up-to-date. During fieldwork, I found buildings, ponds and tracks which were not shown. Such apparitions may cause alarm and confusion, so they are usually mentioned. Some woods and orchards are now fields, and hedges have disappeared. Many small areas of woodland are not indicated. Pubs appear which have, alas, been closed. Most important, footpath diversions, which have obviously been in effect for years, are not shown. The Landranger maps are generally less out-of-date than the Explorer.

Using the guide

Abbreviations

SBP denotes the Sussex Border Path; **OS** Ordnance Survey, and **NT** National Trust. **m/r** is a six-figure OS map (grid) reference.

Waymarking

The SBP is waymarked for most of its length. In West Sussex, there are special wooden signposts. In East Sussex a green and white plate is fixed to existing signposts and to gateposts and stiles. Surrey has a special brown and white waymark sign. Most waymark signs show the Sussex Martlet (a swallow or martin). In Hampshire and Kent, although paths are usually well signposted, there are no special waymarks.

Walks

The most common approach will probably be a series of day walks from a car, with a return to the starting point. For those not returning to their starting point walks can be joined. Many walkers will want to buy lunch *en route*, so each walk includes a pub and where available a cafe or restaurant near its halfway point. For most walks a pub is the only option. Inevitably, the length of the walks varies. If a walk may be too long for some (e.g. round Bewl Wa-

ter) suggestions are made for splitting it. Strong walkers may combine two shorter walks.

Contents of each walk

Sections

Each walk is divided into two or three sections. The first covers the SBP. The second describes an alternative return route (with one exception). If there is no place of refreshment on these two sections a third describes the necessary detour. The most convenient lunch stop is emboldened, e.g. **The Royal Oak.**

There are three sources of information about the route of the SBP: the original guide, OS maps, and signposts and waymarks. Where these differ, I have followed the original guide and mentioned the discrepancy. Most errors are in the OS maps.

Distances

Distances are given for each section of the walk, to the nearest half kilometre and half-mile.

Maps

Explorer and Landranger maps required for the walk.

En route

Places where there are refreshments or shops other than the lunch stop.

Things to see

Places of interest on or near the walk. Details are correct for 1998 but may change.

Parking

Parking is mentioned only when not obvious.

Route descriptions

The OS grid (map) reference of the starting point is given at the appropriate place in the text.

Footpaths and bridleways which cross or diverge from the walk are mentioned only if they provide a landmark, or if there is a risk of confusion. They are usually shown on the sketch maps.

Names of houses, farms, roads, etc. are given to help walkers check their position. Those visible on the ground are used whenever possible. Brackets indicate that the name is not visible at the point where it is first mentioned, e.g. '....take a lane (Brewells Lane)....'. There are many minor discrepancies between the names on maps and the names on signs, and even the same name on two signs. These are indicated thus: Ham (Hamm?).

Paths are generally well signposted, but signposts and waymark posts are not much used as points of reference. They may fall over, be vandalised or maliciously turned to point in the wrong direction. I have seen several places where waymark signs have been wrenched off posts. A farmer told me that his cows often damage waymark signs. I once saw a lorry driver heave a waymark post out of the ground and use it to lever his vehicle out of mud (it was replaced – I checked).

The word *continue* implies *in the same direction*. This should always be assumed; all major changes of direction are mentioned.

There are no real difficulties in following the SBP, apart from nettles and brambles in the summer (shorts have some disadvantages) and the occasional fallen tree. The same is true of the return routes, but only because I altered some of them to avoid difficulties, which you may discover if you try to follow a more obvious way back.

Sketch maps

A sketch map is provided of each walk. The scales vary slightly so that each fits a page without breaks. The suggestion is repeated that OS maps should be used to supplement this guide.

Refreshments and shops

All pubs on or near the walk have been named (and most visited), except in towns. Not all pubs in built-up areas serve food at weekends, and it is best to enquire before ordering drinks. Cafes and restaurants are mentioned when present.

All shops are mentioned, except in towns where their presence may be assumed. Most are small village stores, some in danger of closure. If shops are referred to, it may be assumed that one of them sells food.

Planning

A reasonably fit walker covers three miles (five kilometres) per hour on good level going. Each 10 metres of ascent takes an extra minute. Allow another 5-15 minutes per hour for rests, map-reading and consulting the guide.

These figures do not allow for the notorious Wealden mud, which can reduce progress by a third or more.

Overnight stops

Accommodation

Accommodation of some sort is available at all the towns and larger villages on or near the SBP, but there is not space for details here. The best plan is to ring the nearest Tourist Information Centre (see Useful Addresses).

Many guides are published, but none is exhaustive. The Rambler's Yearbook, free to members, has some useful addresses and maps but at the time of writing (1998) does not indicate those suitable for the SBP.

Youth Hostels

The hosteller is not well served. There are only two hostels near the SBP, at:

Brighton: Patcham Place, London Road, Brighton, BN1 8YD (0.5 km). tel: 01273 556196.

Truleigh Hill: Tottington Barn,

Truleigh Hill, Shoreham-by-Sea, W. Sussex (3 km). tel: 01903 813419.

The figure in brackets is the distance from the SBP.

Camp sites

The table (opposite) is intended mainly for backpackers. It shows camping sites within three kilometres walking distance of the SBP. Many areas have no convenient site and campers will depend on the hospitality of farmers. There is not room to include the many other camping and caravan sites near the SBP. Many guides are available (see useful addresses). The most comprehensive is that published by the Camping and Caravanning Club, on which much of the table is based. Advance booking is usually advisable.

Travel

Bus services

West Sussex

The following Bus Times booklets are available:

Chichester and Bognor Regis; Midhurst; Horsham; Crawley (L); Mid-Sussex (L); Brighton and Hove (L). They are obtainable free of charge from West Sussex County Council (see useful addresses). County Traveline: 0345 959099.

East Sussex

The following Travel Guides include bus timetables:

1. Lewes Area (L); 3. North Wealden (L); 4. Hastings and Rother Area.

They are obtainable free of charge from East Sussex County Council (see

Camp sites

Walk	Town/village Map: L/ranger(L); Explorer (E) Map reference	Address (C&CS = Caravan & Camping Site) Telephone Notes	Distance from SBP
1	Southborne (L)197 (E)120 774056	Chichester C&C Club Site, Main Road, Southborne, Hants, PO10 8JH. 01243 373202.	2.5 km.
1	Emsworth (L)197 (E)120 775058	Loveders Farm C&CS, Inlands Rd, Nutbourne, Nr Chichester, W. Sussex, PO10 8JH. 01243 372368.	3 km.
5	Liphook (L) 186 (E)133 824317	The Deer's Hut, Griggs Green, Longmoor Road, Liphook, GU30 7PD. 01428 724406.	3 km
5	Liphook (L) 186 (E)133 854324	Old Barn Farm, Hewshott Lane, Liphook, GU30 7SY. 01428 722644. *Own sanitation.*	2.5 km
7	Rudgwick (L) 187 (E)134 084343	Canfields Farm, Lynwick St., Rudgwick, W. Sussex, RH12 3DL. 01403 822219. *Own sanitation. No sign on road.*	1 km
10	Charlwood (L)187 (E)146 236404	Windacres Farm, Russ Hill, Charlwood, Horley, Surrey, RH6 OEL. 01293 826092 *Own sanitation.*	on SBP
10	Copthorne (L)187 (E)146 328405	Southern Counties Historic Vehicle Preservation Trust, East Hill Lane, Effingham Rd, Burstow, Surrey. 01737 761800. *Own sanitation. Phone first.*	1.5 km
15	Cousley Wood (L) 188 (E)136 651337	Rainbows End, Newbury Lane, Lower Cousley Wood, Wadhurst, E. Sussex, TN5 6BG. 01892 783791. *Own sanitation. Pitch, owner calls.*	0.5 km
17	Bewl Water (L) 188 (E)136 666337	Ladymeads Farm, Lower Cousley Wood, Wadhurst E. Sussex. 01892 783240 *Own sanitation.*	1 km
17	Flimwell (L) 188 (E) 136. 699332	Stonecrouch Cottage, Stonecrouch, Flimwell. E. Sussex. 01580 8798525.	1 km
17	Flimwell (L)188 (E)136 695336	Cedar Gables, Hastings Rd, Flimwell, Wadhurst, E. Sussex, TN5 7QA. 01892 890566.	1 km
17	Flimwell (L)188 (E)136 703229	Tanner Farm Park, Goudhurst Road, Marden, Tonbridge, Kent TN12 9ND. 01622 832399.	1.5 km.
17	Hurst Green (L) 188, 199 (E) 136 729286	Swanfield Farm House, London Road, Hurst Green, Nr Etchingham, E Sussex, TN19 5JU. 01580 860318.	2 km
18	Bodiam (L) 199 (E)136. 767245	Park Farm C&C, Bodiam, Robertsbridge, E. Sussex. TN32 5XA. 01580 830514.	2.5 km
19	Ewhurst Green (L) 199 (E)125 802227	Lordine Court C&C Park, Ewhurst Green, Staplecross, Robertsbridge, E. Sussex. TN32 5TS. 01580 830209.	2.5km
20	Rye (L) 189 (E)125 915209	Rolvendene Farm, Rye, E. Sussex. 01797 222311. *Own sanitation. Toilets and showers available nearby.*	1 km
22	Danehill (L)187/198 (E)135. 406264	Heaven Farm, Turners Green, Uckfield, TN22 3RG. 01825 790226 *Toilets for campers' use only.*	1 km
23	Sheffield Park (L)198 (E)135. 412244	Sheffield Park Farm, Nr. Uckfield, E. Sussex, TN22 3QR. 01825 790235. *Own sanitation.*	2.5 km
23	Ditchling (L)198 (E)122. 316149	Southdown Farm, Lodge Lane, Keymer, Hassocks, Sussex, BN6 8LX. 01273 843278	1 km

Note: There is a campsite by the car park at Harrison's Rocks, Groombridge for climbers and visitors to the outcrops only.

useful addresses). County Buslines: 01273 474747 for areas 1 and 2, 01797 223053 for area 4.

Mid-Sussex Link

Guides needed are marked (L) above.

General

Services in the more remote areas are very restricted. Many run on only one or two days per week and not at weekends.

Train services

Many places have rail links. Some stations are a long way from the place from which they derive their name; e.g. Wivelsfield.

Preserved railways

There are two near the SBP:

The Bluebell Railway runs close to the SBP, and may be used to reach or return from it. See Walk 21.

The Kent And East Sussex Railway is two kilometres from the SBP at its nearest point at Northiam, and is of no assistance in walking the SBP.

Maps

The maps on pages 8 and 9 show which places have bus and rail services.

Useful addresses and telephone numbers

County Councils

East Sussex County Council: Sackville House, Brooks Close, Lewes, East Sussex, BN7 1VE. tel: 01273 481000

West Sussex County Council: County Hall, Chichester, West Sussex, PO19 1RL. tel: 01243 777100.

Hampshire County Council: Mottisfount Court, High Street, Winchester, SO23 8ZB. tel: 01962 870500.

Surrey County Council: County Hall, Penrhyn Road, Kingston-upon-Thames, KT1 2DN. Tel: 0181 541 9015

Kent County Council; County Hall, Maidstone, ME14 1XQ; tel: 01622 671411

Outdoor organisations

The Camping and Caravanning Club, Greenfields House, Westwood Way, Coventry, CV4 8JH. tel: 01203 694995.

The Caravan Club: East Grinstead House, East Grinstead, West Sussex, RH19 1UA. Tel: 01342 326944.

The Ramblers Association: 1/5 Wandsworth Road, London SW8 2XX. tel: 0171 339 8500.

The Youth Hostels Association: Trevelyan House, 8 St Stephen's Hill, St Albans, Herts, AL1 2DY. Tel: 01727 855215.

Tourist Board

South East England Tourist Board: The Old Brew House, Warwick Park, Tunbridge Wells, Kent, TN2 5TU. tel: 01892 540766.

Tourist Information Centres on or near the SBP

West Sussex

Burgess Hill: 96 Church Walk, RH15 9AS. tel: 01444 247726

Chichester: 29a South Street, PO19 1AH. tel: 01243 775888.

East Grinstead: (Tourist Information

Point) The Library, West Street, RH19 4SR. tel: 01342 410121.

Horsham: 9, Causeway, RH12 1HE. tel: 01403 211661

East Sussex

Brighton: 10 Bartholomew Square, BN1 1JS; tel: 01273 292599.

Hove: Church Road, BN3 3BQ; tel: 01273 292589.

Rye: The Heritage Centre, Strand Quay, TN31 7AY; tel: 01797 226696

Hampshire:

Petersfield: County Library, The Square, GU32 3HH; tel: 01730 268829.

Kent

Tunbridge Wells: The Old Fish Market, The Pantiles, TN2 5TN; tel: 01892 515675.

Surrey

Farnham: Vernon House, 28 West Street, GU7 7DR; tel: 01252 715109.

Guildford: 14 Tunsgate, GU1 3QT; tel: 01483 444333.

Maps

The maps on pages 8 and 9 show which places have Tourist Information Centres.

Travel

Coaches: The telephone number of National Express Coach Enquiries is 0990 808080.

Rail: The telephone number of National Rail Enquiries is 0345 484950.

Books

There are surprisingly few general guide books in print. The Shire County Guide *Sussex* by David J. Allen (no relation) covers both counties and is reasonably priced. There are companion guides for Kent, Surrey and Hampshire. The older Philip's County Guides are good if you can get them. J. R. Armstrong's *History of Sussex* will add interest to many walks and is particularly good on the history of building.

Finally

Parts of this guide will inevitably become out-of-date. During my fieldwork rights of way were diverted, ponds were dug, a massive poultry house was erected and a house and a brick tower – both useful landmarks – were demolished. Information about changes, and other comments or criticisms, will be welcome.

You will not find exhortations to use care when crossing roads. It is assumed that anyone discriminating enough to buy this guide has enough sense to do so without gratuitous advice. Instructions to cross a stile need not be taken literally if there is an open gate beside it. Nor is it necessary to pass a pub because the guide tells you to.

I hope you enjoy walking the SBP as much as I did.

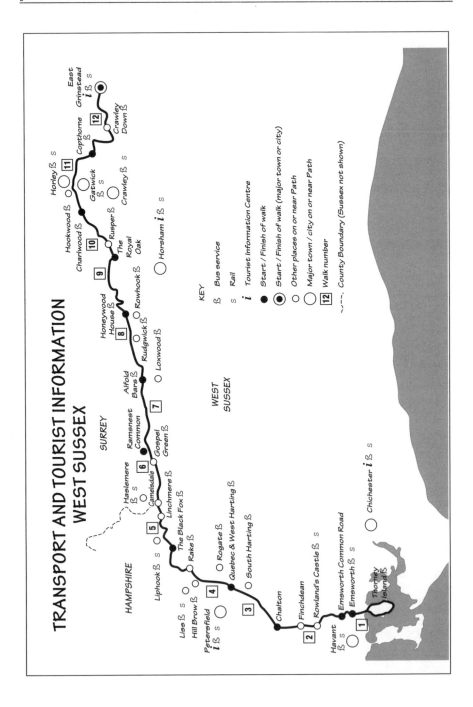

TRANSPORT AND TOURIST INFORMATION
WEST SUSSEX

KEY

ß   Bus service
S   Rail
i   Tourist Information Centre
●   Start / Finish of walk
⊙   Start / Finish of walk (major town or city)
○   Other places on or near Path
◯   Major town / city on or near Path
12   Walk number
~·~ County Boundary (Sussex not shown)

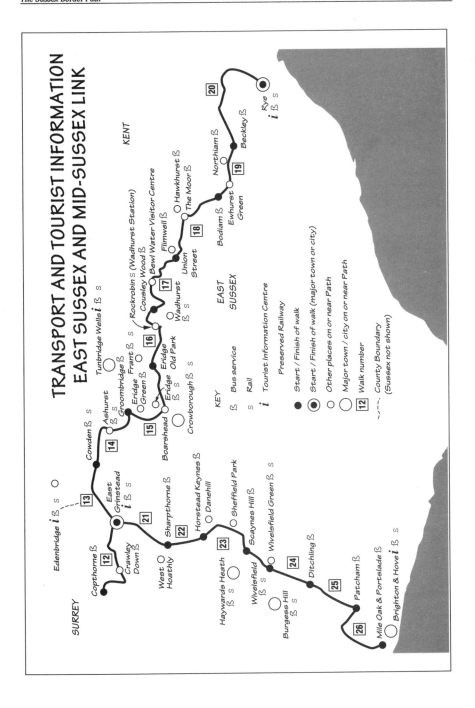

TRANSPORT AND TOURIST INFORMATION
EAST SUSSEX AND MID-SUSSEX LINK

KEY

ß Bus service

s Rail

i Tourist Information Centre

▬▬ Preserved Railway

● Start / Finish of walk

◉ Start / Finish of walk (major town or city)

○ Other places on or near Path

◯ Major town / city on or near Path

[12] Walk number

‒ · ‒ · County Boundary
(Sussex not shown)

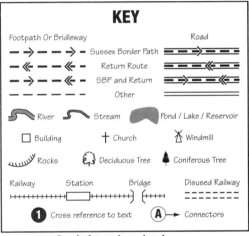

KEY

Footpath Or Bridleway   Road

Sussex Border Path

Return Route

SBP and Return

Other

River   Stream   Pond / Lake / Reservoir

Building   Church   Windmill

Rocks   Deciduous Tree   Coniferous Tree

Railway   Station   Bridge   Disused Railway

1 Cross reference to text   A Connectors

Symbols used on sketch maps

West Sussex

North-west shore, Thorney Island – Walk 1

1. Thorney Island to Emsworth Common Road

Distance: SBP: Thorney Island: 10.5 km, 6.5 miles (circular walk).
Emsworth Common walk: 6 km; 3.5 miles. **Return:** 4km, 2.5 miles.

Maps: Explorer 120; Landranger 197.

En route: *Emsworth:* shops and pubs.

Things to see: *Thorney Island:* Church of St Nicholas: XII century;
Nature Reserves. *Emsworth*: Museum: Easter to Sep, Sat 1000-1600,
Sun 1400-1600. *Westbourne:* Church of St John Baptist.

These two walks can be done on the same day.

Thorney Island

Thorney Island really was an island until 1870, when sea-walls were built and the area which now connects it to the mainland was drained. This area, north of Great Deep, is now a Nature Reserve, and includes a salt marsh with rare flora and fauna. The larger southern section is owned by the MOD, as many threatening notices remind you. A disused airfield occupies most of this area, with some agricultural land on the west.

The paths round the island are well signposted, but there are no special SBP waymarks. The walk is described clockwise. It is utterly flat, as are most of the views, and makes for fast going. It is the only part of the SBP where you walk by the sea.

1. SBP: From Slipper Mill Pond (753058), walk along the south side of the road towards Chichester. Just past the Old Bakery, take a footpath on the right, first between houses and then along the edge of a field with a lot of brambles. Continue

along the edge of another field to a house with a wooden seat outside. Just past here move right into the marina and continue along a path. At a sign *Harbour Office* move right again and continue past deckhouses (elevated to provide views) on the right. Opposite number 8, take a stile on the left and cross a field. Cross a road and follow a path along the edges of fields. At Thornham Farm take the left-hand of two gravel drives and continue along a private road to a Sea Scout headquarters.

2. From this point no guidance is needed, as the SBP follows the shoreline for a long way. Turn right and follow the path along the sea wall and through Payne's New Quay Marina. At Great Deep, MOD property begins. To gain admission you speak to a disembodied voice – the response may not be immediate. At West Thorney, the path passes the Church of St Nicholas, where there are graves of German servicemen. At Thorney Island Sailing Club the path descends to the foreshore for a short distance; there is a High Water alter-

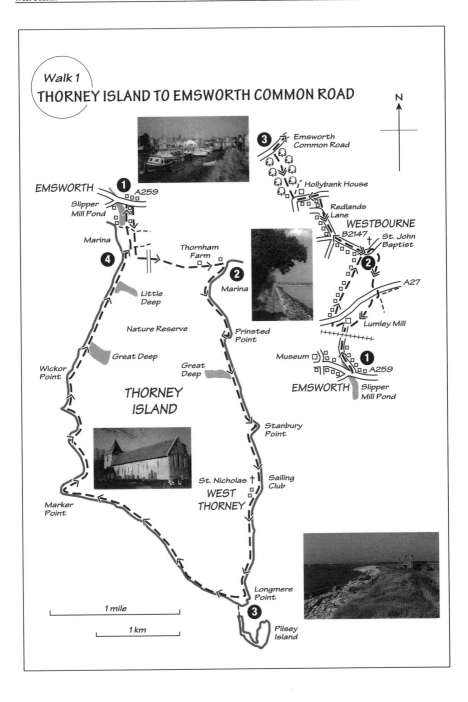

Walk 1
THORNEY ISLAND TO EMSWORTH COMMON ROAD

N

3 Emsworth Common Road

Hollybank House

EMSWORTH **1** A259

Slipper Mill Pond

Redlands Lane

WESTBOURNE
B2147 † St. John Baptist

Marina

4 Thornham Farm

2

2

A27

Little Deep

Marina

Nature Reserve

Prinsted Point

Lumley Mill

Great Deep

Great Deep

Museum

1

Wickor Point

THORNEY ISLAND

EMSWORTH Slipper Mill Pond A259

Stanbury Point

St. Nicholas † Sailing Club

WEST THORNEY

Marker Point

Longmere Point

1 mile

1 km

3

Pilsey Island

native which starts between the church and the club building.

3. Longmere Point is the southern extremity of the island, and from it there is limited access to another Nature Reserve on Pilsey Island. At Great Deep, another dialogue with the disembodied voice is necessary, unless the gate has been left open, as on one of my visits. Continue along a straight stretch for over a kilometre, after which directions become necessary again.

4. Bear left for a short distance along the shore, and just past deckhouses take a path on the right. Walk by moorings for a short distance, then turn left beside them and continue past the offices and the Slipper Mill building to a road. Continue with Slipper Mill Pond on the left to the A259. There are two pubs, the **Lord Raglan** on the left and the **Millpond** straight ahead.

Slipper Mill Pond to Emsworth Common Road

This is a pleasant short walk, rather better than the map suggests.

1. SBP: From the A259 walk along Lumley Road, with Emsworth Creek on the left (OS Explorer maps show the SBP on the other side, possibly due to an error, since corrected, in the original guide). Continue under a railway bridge and, just before the end of the road, take a path on the left and cross a stream near sluice gates. Follow the path back towards the railway and at a gas installation turn back to the right and follow a path under the A27. There seems no justification for the SBP blob *south* of the

railway on the Explorer map. Go through a long field, cross a stile on the left just before its end and continue to the B2147 (Westbourne Road).

2. Turn left and continue to a mini-roundabout. Bear right along Redlands Lane. Where the road swings left keep straight on along a path (which is still Redlands Lane). Continue along a track to a road, turn left, and follow it until it swings left at Hollybank House. Turn right along a track into a wood and continue to Emsworth Common Road.

3. Return: Walk back to, and along, the B2147. Instead of turning right along the SBP, continue into Westbourne. Just before the church take a path on the right beside a stream. Continue along a track, round to the left and over the A27. Turn right along a track and follow it back to re-join the SBP by Lumley Mill.

2. Emsworth Common Road to Chalton

Distance: SBP: 10 km, 6 miles. **Return:** 11 km, 6.5 miles.

Maps: Explorer 120, Landranger 197.

En route: *Rowlands Castle:* pubs, shops, café; *Finchdean:* pub.

Parking: limited space at two points where SBP meets road. Larger area halfway between.

Things to see: *Chalton:* Church of St. Michael and All Angels. *Stansted Park:* Wren-style house, ancient chapel, walled garden, arboretum, parkland: Easter-Sep, Sun, Mon, 1400-1730; house: bank holidays and Jul, Aug, Sun, Mon, 1400-1730; tel: 01705 412265. *Idsworth:* Church of St Hubert.

This is a walk of contrasts which begins in level woodland and parkland and then climbs a ridge of the South Downs. Part of the walk is shared with the Staunton Way.

---

1. SBP: From the point where Walk 1 meets the road (743084), turn right and walk east for half a kilometre. Take a path on the left through Shuffle's Plantation, where a stream can give problems after heavy rain. Cross Woodberry Lane and continue through woodland and fields. At Holme Farm turn left between stables, then right and left at the end of the farm buildings to continue along a track. Continue past Lyeis Wood to a junction of tracks just before Horsepasture Farm. Turn right and follow a path towards a section of fence at the edge of a wood.

2. Turn left along a broad grassy ride, The Avenue, which leads to Stansted House. At the end, continue along a path on the right. Cross a footbridge and a track to Finchdean Road. To visit Rowland's Castle, turn left. For the SBP turn right and continue until the road swings gently to the left.

3. Take a path on the left, go uphill to garages, turn right beside the railway and then left under it. Walk uphill towards a red brick house and bear left to follow a track past the house. Turn right by Wellsworth Farm and bear right into a field. This section of the SBP is shared by the Staunton Way. Views of the South Downs open up ahead, and Idsworth House can be seen on the left. At the end of the field continue to a road and go downhill into Finchdean.

4. Walk past The George and turn left along a road signposted *Chalton*. By Ashcroft Lane cross a stile on the right and follow a path parallel to the road. At the corner of the field turn right uphill. Go through Oxleys Copse and turn left, then right just before the crest of the hill. There are fine views north and east, where Uppark can be seen just below the skyline.

Stansted House

5. The path leaves the wood to run between fields. Not far from the wood cross a stile on the left and follow a path which veers away from the fence. Continue over the brow of the hill by tumuli, and go gently downhill to an old hedge where three paths converge. Bear left and then right through the graveyard of the church at Chalton. Cross a small green to **The Red Lion Inn**, a thatched building whose origins go back to the XII century (see the menu). Chalton is a beautiful little village high on a ridge.

6. Return: Retrace your steps to the junction of the three paths and take the middle one. Go diagonally downhill through uncultivated land. Continue just above a fence and follow it round to the left to a stile. Turn right and follow a path just below a fence. At the corner of a field, turn left and go down to a railway bridge. Turn right and follow a path to a road. Turn right and continue past a lane, and then past the track leading to St Huberts. Continue to a drive on the left to Old Idsworth Garden.

7. Take a path to the left of the drive and go past the house to a wood. Turn right and follow a path along its edge, keeping right at a fork. Cross a field, trending uphill, and the corner of another, then turn left along a track. Continue past a house, and turn left at a T-junction in front of South Holt Farm. Pass to the left of the farmhouse, turn right along a track, follow it downhill to a house and turn left along another track. Almost immediately, take a path on the

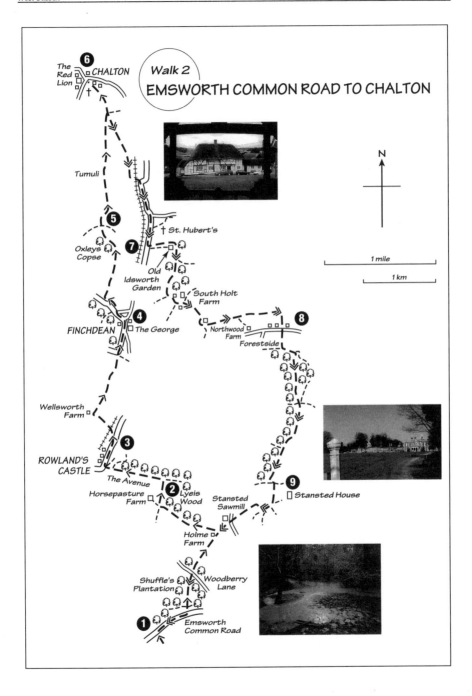

Walk 2

EMSWORTH COMMON ROAD TO CHALTON

The Red Lion

6 CHALTON

Tumuli

5

Oxleys Copse

7

† St. Hubert's

Old Idsworth Garden

South Holt Farm

4

FINCHDEAN □ The George

Northwood Farm

Forestside

8

Wellsworth Farm

3

ROWLAND'S CASTLE

The Avenue

Horsepasture Farm

2 Lyeis Wood

Stansted Sawmill

9 □ Stansted House

Holme Farm

Shuffle's Plantation

Woodberry Lane

1 Emsworth Common Road

N

1 mile

1 km

St Michael and All Angels, Chalton

right at a slight angle to the track. Go uphill to join a track, and continue past Northwood Farm, 300 metres on the right. By a small wood on the left take a stile on the right, and follow a path to the road at Forestside.

8. Turn left and almost immediately right across a field to a wood. The way through the wood is tricky but well signposted. Turn left along the edge of the wood and then right at its corner. Continue into the wood, crossing another path. Where the path meets a track bear left along the path and follow it round to the right. Bear right where a path joins from the left, and shortly keep straight on across a track. Keep left at a fork along a grassy path and continue to the edge of the wood. Turn right and continue beside the wood for over a kilometre, to the drive to Stansted House. Turn left and then right, by a small wood, along a path which runs in front of the house.

9. Turn right along another drive and follow it to double wooden gates on the right. Take a path beside these and follow it round to the left. Cross the road by Stansted Sawmill and follow a track to Holme Farm, then follow the SBP back to the start.

3. Chalton to Quebec

Distance: SBP: 8 km, 5 miles. **Return:** 12 km, 7.5 miles.

Maps: Explorer 120, Landranger 197.

Things to see: *South Harting:* Church of St. Mary and St. Gabriel: XIV century. *Uppark:* (NT) Wren-style house, garden, fully restored after 1989 fire, Apr-Oct, Sun-Thu, 1300-1700, tel: 01730 825415.

This walk is mainly downland, with a flattish section north of the escarpment. Unusually the return, which includes a long section of the South Downs Way, is better than the outward walk.

---

1. SBP: From The Red Lion (731160), walk to a grass triangle and follow a lane signposted *Ditcham, Idsworth, Compton.* Pass a byway, turn left through a gap into a field, and follow a path downhill. Cross two metal stiles and go steeply downhill, bearing left along a faint path. Cross another metal stile to a lane by Woodcroft House. Turn left and then right over the railway, then turn right past Woodcroft Farm. Cross a private road and bear left along a track which immediately forks. Take the right fork, which is signposted as an off-road cycle track. Follow this track (Harris Lane) along the bottom of a pleasant valley, mainly between woodland. The track swings gently left and a bridle-way joins from the right, below Ladyholt.

2. A little further on, the track forks. Keep right for a long uphill trudge, between deciduous trees on the left and evergreens on the right. The track levels and a more prominent track joins from the right and continues ahead. Turn left here, along a grassy path which first goes slightly uphill and then levels out. Cross a

track and continue downhill, where the path joins a track. This track joins another and enters open country at Foxcombe House, which is much more prominent than the Foxcombe Farm named on the map. The track joins a metalled lane. Continue past Foxcombe Cottages and cross the South Downs Way at Downlands. The ruined tower on Tower Hill is well seen on the right. Follow the lane downhill and cross the B2146.

3. Take a path which runs beside a lane along the base of Torberry Hill. Where the path joins the lane keep left, signposted *Rogate.* Keep right at a fork, again signposted *Rogate,* and continue past Collins Lane on the right. Continue to another junction.

4. Return: Turn back to the right and follow the lane through West Harting, passing lanes on the right and left. At a junction below Torberry Hill keep left, signposted *South Harting.* Pass a path on the left and take a grassy path on the right to the B2146. Cross and follow a track to Church Farm. Turn left along a path before the farm buildings and

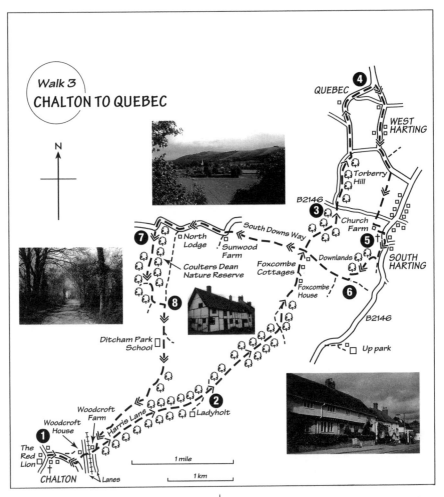

Walk 3

CHALTON TO QUEBEC

N

QUEBEC

WEST HARTING

Torberry Hill

B2146

Church Farm

South Downs Way

North Lodge

Sunwood Farm

Coulters Dean Nature Reserve

Foxcombe Cottages

Downlands

SOUTH HARTING

Foxcombe House

B2146

Up park

Ditcham Park School

Woodcroft Farm

Harris Lane

Ladyholt

Woodcroft House

The Red Lion

CHALTON

Lanes

1 mile

1 km

follow it round a right turn to a drive. Turn left and continue to **South Harting**.

If you turn left you will come to The White Hart, public toilets, The Ship and the village stores. This western part of the village has houses of several different styles and ages, but the eastern part contains only modern housing estates.

5. Turn right up the B2146 past the church, and where the road bends left keep straight on into public gardens. Walk to the far end, where there are several paths, and take the most obvious one, going straight on uphill. Keep right where a path goes off left. Just past a wooden seat take a path on the right and follow it uphill through a wood. At a junction of paths keep right, then left at the next

The White Hart, South Harting

junction. The path follows the edge of the wood and does not cross a field as may be shown on your map. Continue to a stile on the left and walk up to the South Downs Way.

6. After a pause to enjoy the views, turn right and follow the Way for over three kilometres, crossing the SBP and the West Sussex border, where the Way used to end before it was extended into Hampshire. At Sunwood Farm turn left and right along a lane and continue past a private road which forks off to the left. The lane turns left and then right.

7. At this point take a path on the left into Coulters Dean Nature Reserve, and follow it along the edge of a wood. Continue gently uphill into Ditcham Wood, which is preserved rather than conserved. At the top of

the ridge the path first crosses a track and then joins it at a curve. Turn right and follow the track along the ridge. Where the track goes away to the right at the corner of a field turn left along a path. Follow the path over the ridge and down to the private road to Ditcham Park School.

8. Turn right along the road and where it swings right keep straight on along a track. Pass the school on your right, enjoying excellent views south. Follow the track down to Woodcroft Farm and follow the SBP back to Chalton.

4. Quebec to The Black Fox

Distance: SBP: 13 km, 8 miles. **Return:** 10.5 km, 6.5 miles

Maps: Explorer 133, Landranger 197.

Parking: on the road between the start and West Harting.

En route: *Hill Brow:* pub; *Rake:* pub, shop.

This walk provides a mixture of farmland, woodland and heathland. There is rather more road work than usual, mostly along quiet lanes. There are few extensive views until the final stages of the return, when the South Downs loom ahead. The walk can be split at Rake.

1. SBP: From the junction (782216), follow the lane north and take a path on the right just before a wood. Walk beside the wood to a footbridge on the left and in the next field turn left over a stile. Cross a field, keeping to the left of a pylon, and continue across the next. Cross a footbridge and bear right towards Down Park Farm. Turn right along a metalled track and then left by a metal tower, along another track. Where this swings right continue along a path over West Heath Common. Bear left to join a track and turn right through the dismantled bridge of an old railway. Pass a house and continue along the edge of a field to join a track. Follow this for a short distance, then bear right across a field to a farm bridge over the River Rother. Continue along a track to the A272 by Wenham Manor Farm.

2. Turn left and walk along the road. Turn right along a track to Durleighmarsh Farm and follow it uphill to the farm, which has a good shop. Keep left at the top, continue to the corner of Durford Wood, and take

a path to the right along the edge of the wood. Continue through the wood, keeping left at a fork where a track runs beside the path. Continue along the bottom of the valley to join a track and follow it to a road.

3. Turn left. If you continue along the road you will soon come to the Jolly Drover at Hill Brow. For the SBP, walk a short distance along the road, then take a road on the right sign-posted *Milland.* Follow the road downhill until it swings right and take the left-hand of two tracks. After 300 metres take a path on the left which climbs gently away from the track, and continue to a road. Turn left uphill to the B2070 and The Flying Bull at Rake.

4. If you turn left along the B2070 you will soon come to The Sun Inn and a shop. For the SBP, cross the road and take a lane (Brewells Lane) beside the Flying Bull. Fork right at signpost *Brewells* and follow another lane. At Oak Hanger turn right, continue to a T-junction and turn left. This lane ends just over a railway bridge, where there are three tracks.

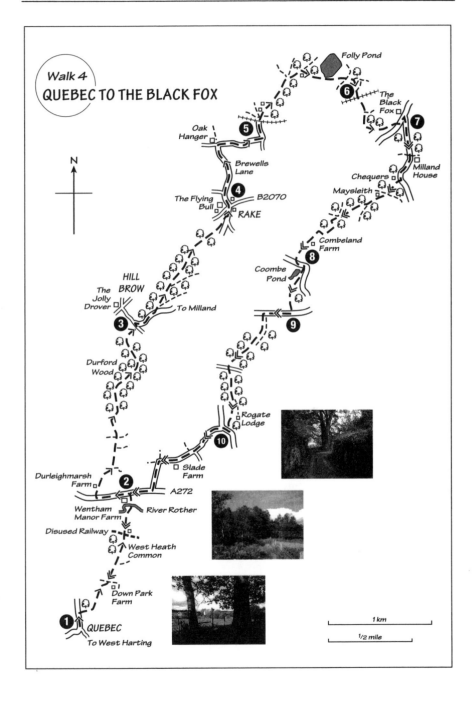

Walk 4
QUEBEC TO THE BLACK FOX

Folly Pond

The Black Fox

6

7

Oak Hanger

5

Brewells Lane

Chequers

Milland House

Maysleith

N

The Flying Bull

4

B2070

RAKE

Combeland Farm

8

Coombe Pond

HILL BROW

The Jolly Drover

3

To Milland

9

Durford Wood

Rogate Lodge

10

Slade Farm

Durleighmarsh Farm

2

A272

Wentham Manor Farm

River Rother

Disused Railway

West Heath Common

Down Park Farm

1

QUEBEC

To West Harting

1 km

½ mile

The Sussex Border Path above Durleighmarsh Farm near Petersfield

5. Take the one on the right (but not the one which immediately goes off right from this one). Just past some cottages, the track shrinks to a path. Continue with a wood on the right. At a junction of paths, where the corner of one wood meets the corner of another, turn right and go downhill through the wood. Cross a track by cottages and follow a path along the edge of a wood. From the map, you would expect to see Folly Pond on the left, but the trees allow only glimpses. For those not sufficiently exercised by the walk, there are parts of a fitness trail beside the path. At a metalled lane, a brief detour may be made to the left to visit Folly Pond, attractively set amongst pine and silver birch trees.

6. Just past the lane fork right and then bear right, keeping near the edge of the wood. Go under a railway bridge and take a path on the left, which swings to the right away from the railway. Continue between fields into woodland and immediately turn right. At the next junction, keep left. Cross a track and go past houses to the B2070 and the **Black Fox Inn** (accommodation).

7. Return: From the inn turn left, and immediately sharply right along a minor road signposted *Milland*. Follow the road downhill and to the right, then take a tarmac track on the right, with a sign *Chequers*, and follow it round to the left. At Maysleith, continue along a track below the house. Continue through woodland

and then along the edge of open ground (which the map may show as woodland) on the left. Where the open ground narrows, go down to a track on the left (there is a signpost at this point) and continue downhill with woodland on the left. Go uphill for a short distance to a gate on the left. Cross the corner of a field to a gate on the right, and turn right into woodland. Follow the path right and left to join a track at Combeland Farm and continue to a lane.

8. Turn left and, just before the road bends right, take a path on the right by a small private car park. Follow the path to the left of Coombe Pond. A little before the end of the pond take a path on the left and follow it through a wood. At the end of the wood cross a stile on the left and follow the right edge of a field to a road.

9. Turn right and continue to a track on the left, with a sign *Fyning Hill Estate*. The right of way runs just to the right of this track. The next section may appear complex, but signposts and Private signs make it easy to follow the correct route. At the top of a rise bear right and right again by a bend in the drive. Follow the path as its winds uphill through woodland, cross a track, and turn left at a junction of paths. At the top of the hill cross a public road and continue downhill along a path. Pass a path going uphill to the right and just past here fork right. Keep right at the next fork and continue to the drive to Rogate Lodge. Turn right and follow the drive to a road.

10. Turn right and shortly take a lane on the left, which gives good views to the South Downs. Keep right at a junction and continue past Slade Farm. Turn left at the next junction and then right along the A272. At Wenham Manor Farm turn left and follow the SBP back to the start.

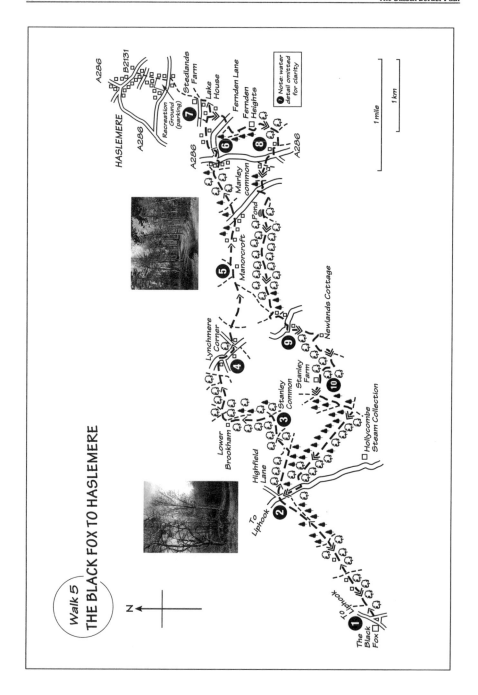

Walk 5
THE BLACK FOX TO HASLEMERE

5. The Black Fox to Haslemere

Distance: SBP: 9 km, 5.5 miles. **Return:** 10.5 km, 6.5 miles. **Haslemere:** 3 km, 2 miles

Maps: Explorer 133, Landranger 186.

En route: *A286:* restaurant.

Things to see: *Hollycombe Steam Collection:* Edwardian fairground, traction engines, railways, Easter -11 Oct, Sunday and bank hols, daily end Jul and end Aug, tel: 01428 724900.

Much of this section of the SBP, and almost the entire return, runs through woodland. Fortunately this is natural and much more pleasant than the gloomy ranks of commercial forests. The walk is hilly, but trees allow only an occasional view.

1. SBP: From the Black Fox (829290), cross the main road and a minor road, signposted *Milland* and *Iping.* Follow a track north-east for nearly two kilometres, through a golf course, past large houses and through woodland. At the end of a field on the left, fork left along a path to a road junction.

2. Cross the road to Highfield Lane and immediately turn right along a path through woodland. Follow the most obvious path until, just past a fallen branch which has been sawn through to allow passage, fork left, slightly uphill. The path joins a track. Follow this until it swings sharply right and continue along a path. Follow the path down into a valley and a junction of paths and turn left.

3. A signpost correctly shows the SBP going along the valley, but your map may show it going up the hill and down the ridge. Above a large house (Lower Brookham), the path

swings to the right and soon there is a junction of five paths. Take the second on the right and go uphill through an area of open ground. At the top of the hill turn right and continue, over a path which crosses diagonally, to a road at Lynchmere Corner.

4. Turn right and follow the road round past Danley Lane, then turn left along a lane signposted *Haslemere* and *Camelsdale.* Just past the house at this corner take a track on the right. Continue along a path, gently uphill between fields and woods to a private road. Follow this for a short distance to Manorcroft, and take a track on the right.

5. Continue through woodland and over a drive to a lane. Turn left and then right at a car park onto Marley Common (NT). Follow the obvious path across the common, round to the right and downhill. A little way down the hill, take a path on the left going more steeply downhill. Cross a

Marley Common

minor road and continue to the A286 by Shrimpton's Licensed Restaurant.

6. Turn left along the A286 and cross to Fernden Lane. Follow the lane round to the left, and where it swings right take a track on the left. Follow this track round to the right and continue along a path, a private road and another path. At a private road turn right past Vine Cottage and then left. Go under a brick arch into the grounds of Lake House. Above the house turn left, cross a wooden walkway over marshy ground and follow the path beside the grounds of the house.

Haslemere: To visit the town, cross a footbridge to Stedlands Farm. Turn right in front of the house, take the left-hand of two footpaths, and go uphill to a road. Turn left and almost immediately right along a tarmac path. Follow the path over a minor road to the B2131, turn left and walk into Haslemere, where there are shops, restaurants and a pub, the White Horse – surprisingly, the only one.

7. Return: Retrace your steps round Lake House and along the private road to Greensleeves. Take a path on the left and walk uphill to Fernden Lane. Turn right, walk past Appletrees, turn left into a drive and immediately left along a path. Continue along a private road to a T-junction and turn left into Fernden Heights Private Estate. Take a drive on the right, signposted *The Lodge*, and by this house take a path on the right. Follow this downhill to the left and at the bottom turn right and cross an old dam. Continue to a fork, keep right, and then turn right along another path. Continue along a private road and turn right at a T-junction to the A286.

8. Turn right and shortly take a footpath on the left. At a track turn left and immediately right along a narrow path beside Rose Cottage. Continue strenuously uphill, cross a track and continue to a lane. Turn right and just before a car park (from which there is a splendid view) take a footpath going sharply back to the left onto Marley Common. Follow the path downhill and take another path downhill to the right. Keep left at a fork and by a brick-lined pond fork right. Almost immediately turn right along a track and follow it round to the left. Continue west along this track, which shrinks to a path, for a kilometre and a half. Just after it swings 90 degrees to the right, turn sharply back to the left along a path, with a tennis court on the right. By a house bear right along a path and at the next house turn right along a gravel drive. At a T-junction keep straight on along a path to a lane.

9. Turn right along the road and then left down a drive with a sign *Newlands Cottage*. Follow the drive to the cottage, and bear right past its garage along a path. Follow this round to the left to join another path and keep straight on where a path goes off right. By a sweet chestnut with two trunks, take a path on the right going steeply uphill. At the top of the steep section, turn left along a track and follow it sharply round to the right and then to the left past Stanley Farm.

10. Where the farm track swings right, turn left along another into woodland. Keep right at a fork and continue gently uphill through double wooden gates. Just past these turn left at a T-junction (which may not be shown on your map). Continue past a track on the left, then turn right at a T-junction and go straight downhill for over a kilometre, along a track which finally swings left to a road. Turn right, walk back to Highfield Lane and turn left to follow the SBP back to The Black Fox.

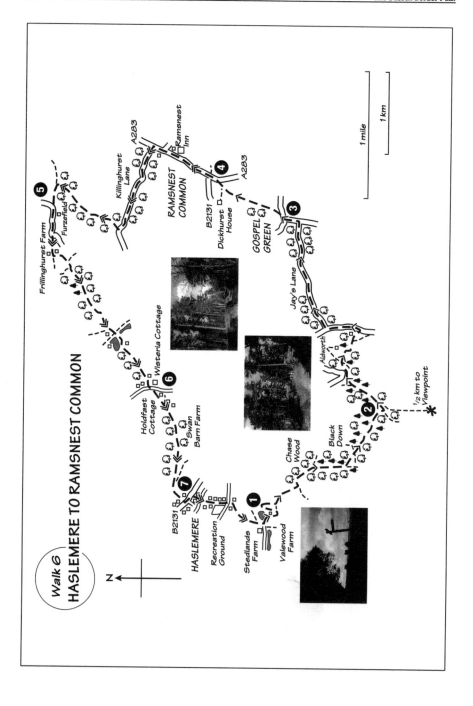

Walk 6
HASLEMERE TO RAMSNEST COMMON

6. Haslemere to Ramsnest Common

Distance: SBP: 7 Km, 4.5 miles. **Return:** 8.5 km. 5.5 miles.

Maps: Explorer 133, Landranger 186.

Parking: is not possible on the narrow lane to Stedlands Farm. There is a public car park at the recreation ground (entrance 905321) in the road above, which is on the return route (see map).

Although this walk is short, it includes an ascent of Black Down, at 918' (280m) the highest point in Sussex, and time should be allowed for a detour to its viewpoint. The pinewoods are superb, as are the views.

---

1. SBP: If you begin at the Recreation Ground, turn left along the road and shortly take a path on the right. Just south of Stedlands Farm (903316), follow a track signposted *Valewood Farm House*. Just past the grounds of the house, take a track on the left which doubles back above the house, and doubles back again along the top of a field. Follow the path across the next field, and turn left into Chase Wood. At the top of the hill take the right fork. Continue to a fork in the path, where there is a waymark post, and go uphill to the left. At the top of the ridge, where the path joins another, turn right. Cross another path and continue along the ridge. This is Black Down, the former site of beacon fires and a semaphore station. A path joins from the left, and there is a junction of four tracks.

2. It is worth making a detour at this point to the viewpoint at the southern end of the ridge, by following a winding track south for a kilometre. For the SBP, turn left and go gently uphill, with fine views appearing on the right. Continue towards a notice board and a pillar which looks like a trig point but isn't and just before these turn right downhill. At a hairpin bend in a lane, there is a private road to Aldworth. Take a path which first runs beside this road, then crosses a track and goes downhill, swinging right and left. Near the bottom of the hill fork left above a large house and continue to a lane. Turn left and follow the lane to a junction. Turn right and follow Jay's Lane to a T-junction, then turn left to another T-junction at Gospel Green.

3. Cross the road and take a path into a wood. Continue through the wood to the drive to Dickhurst House, and turn right to the A283. Turn left to its junction with the B2131.

4. Return: Continue along the A283 to **The Ramsnest Inn** (Ram's Nest?) at Ramsnest Common. From the inn, continue north to Killinghurst Lane on the left, and follow it for a kilometre until it swings sharply left at the corner of a wood. Take a path on the right into the wood and continue along its edge. Cross a footbridge and

Walkers on Black Down, the highest point in Sussex and on the SBP

the pond, and follow a private road past farm buildings to a lane by Wisteria Cottage.

6. Turn left and immediately right along a path beside Holdfast Cottage. Follow this to a stile on the left by some large houses. Continue along a path into woodland and into Swan Barn Farm (NT). Follow the edge of a field, cross a footbridge, and continue along the edge of another field. Cross a footbridge in a strip of woodland and follow the edge of a field into Witley Copse and Mariners Rewe (also NT). The obvious path from this point does not follow the right of way on the map. Follow the path through the wood, cross a footbridge and fork left. Fork left again near the edge of the wood to a footbridge. Bear right across a field, turn right along a track and follow it round to the B2131.

fork left, ignoring a smaller path to the left. Bear left, and keep left where the path meets another. At the edge of the wood turn left and continue to a lane.

5. Turn left past Furzefield, and continue to a drive on the right to Frillinghurst Farm. Go through the farm buildings and just past them take a stile on the left. Cross a field and two stiles. Cross the corner of the next field (which may appear as woodland on older maps) and continue along its lower edge, with a wood on the left. Go into the wood, cross a footbridge and continue along the obvious path into more open country, with views of Black Down on the left. Continue along the edge of a field. Just before a large house, move left into the adjoining field and continue to a track by a large pond. Turn left and right round

7. Turn left past Museum Hill and opposite The Old Manse turn right along the footpath used to reach Haslemere from Walk 5, which leads to the recreation ground. To reach the SBP at Stedlands Farm, turn left along the road and shortly take a path on the right.

7. Ramsnest Common to Alfold Bars

Distance: SBP: 10.5 km, 6.5 miles. **Return:** 12.5 km, 8 miles.

Maps: Explorer 133 and 134, Landranger 186.

En route: *Shillinglee Golf Club:* refreshments.

Parking: on verges A283 just south of start.

This walk is not hilly, but there are good views, particularly in the early stages. There are many wooded sections which can be muddy. The return follows the Wey South Path for some distance.

---

1. SBP: Cross the A283 opposite the B2131 (946324), and go along the edge of a field into a wood. Immediately keep left at a fork and continue through the wood into a field. Follow its edge into another wood and cross a path. Follow the right edge of a series of four fields, bearing round to the right, to a lane at Garden Cottage. The Shillinglee Golf Club on the right welcomes walkers to use its bars, toilets and restaurant.

2. Cross the lane, take a path to the left of Garden Cottage and follow a fence round to the right. Turn left and follow a path between fences, soon with the golf course on the right. Continue along the edge of a field, and in the next cross to the other side of a hedge. Continue along the edge of a wood and along the edge of three fields with Downlands Wood on the left. At the corner of the third field, turn into the wood and follow a path along its edge. At a junction of paths move back into a field and continue with the wood on the left, bearing round to the left. Continue through a wood and then along a gravel drive and a track be-

tween houses. By a metalled road on the right, keep straight on along a path. This briefly joins a track; when this swings left just before a lane, continue along the path.

3. Cross a road to a track to Dungate Cottage and follow it round to the right past farm buildings. Continue along the edge of a field into a wood. Continue along a track, and near the corner of a field turn left and almost immediately right along a path, and follow it round to the right. Where another path crosses, turn left and go gently downhill to join a track. Follow the track to a Y-junction, where there is an isolated Scots Pine, and turn left along a path. At the corner of a field turn right. The path joins a track by Lee House Farm. Follow this through Hog Wood until it swings right by Forest View.

4. Turn left along a path beside a house. Continue between fields, along the edge of a wood and through fields to Barberry Bridge. Continue along the edge of a wood and through fields to Oakhurst Farm. Follow a track past the farm buildings and continue to a lane. Turn left and walk

The SBP by Downlands Wood east of Haslemere

to the **Sir Roger Tichborne** at Alfold Bars.

It was the disappearance of Sir Roger that led to the famous Tichborne Case, when the 24-stone Claimant optimistically asserted that he was the missing 9-stone baronet. Although unsuccessful, and subsequently imprisoned, he attracted a lot of support, and some still believe his claim was genuine.

5. Return: Follow the SBP back past Oakhurst Farm into a strip of woodland just before Barberry Bridge. Turn right along the Wey South Path and follow the course of the old canal to High Bridge (a house).

6. Turn right past the house and immediately left, and follow a track

which bears away from the canal through Sidney Wood. Ignore a path on the right, cross a track and continue to a lane by Old Knightons. Follow the lane past Knightons (a different building) and just before houses on either side of the road turn left into a field. Bear right along its edge, cross a strip of woodland and then a field to the right of a barn. Cross a stile and turn right along a grassy track to a lane.

7. Turn left past Hurlands, continue to the end of the lane and keep straight on along a track past farm buildings on the right. Follow the track as it winds downhill and straightens out to pass Burningfold Manor. Where the track swings right

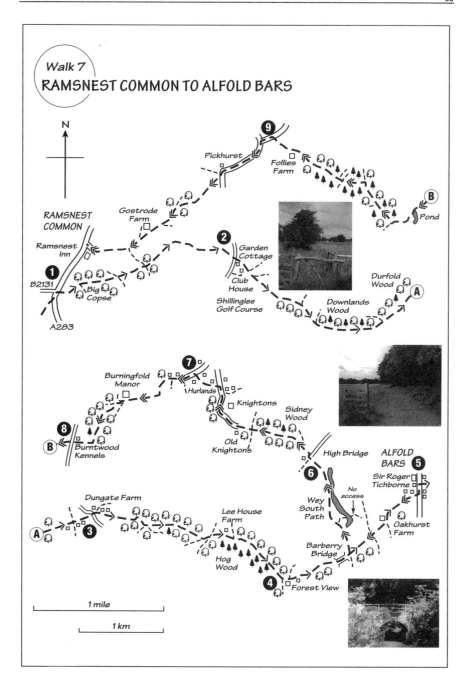

Walk 7
RAMSNEST COMMON TO ALFOLD BARS

towards the buildings, keep straight on along a grassy track and fork left to pass a circular wooden enclosure on your right. Cross a stile into a wood, cross a track and continue along a faint path. Just past a field on the right, turn right and continue to a road by Burntwood Kennels.

8. Cross a stile almost opposite and follow the edge of a field into a wood. Continue along an awkward path. Bear left over a footbridge, follow a faint path through the wood, cross another footbridge and continue along the edge of a field to a pond. Cross the dam and continue halfway along the edge of another field, then cross a stile on the right into a wood. Turn left and then right along the edge of the wood. Cross a stile and turn right along a made track. Keep straight on at a T-junction of tracks, ascend and descend a slight rise, and where the track swings right take a path on the left. Follow this to another track, and keep right where a path joins from the left. Continue beside a field on the right and go through the garden of Follies Farm. Continue along the drive to a road.

9. Turn left and left again at a T-junction, signposted *Fisher Lane*. Where the road bends left at Pickhurst, ignore a bridleway on the right and a little further on take a footpath on the same side. Cross a field to a stile and continue uphill across a field. At the top of the rise, where there are good views of Black Down, bear right to a stile. Bear left across a field (which may be shown as woodland on older maps) to a stile, turn left along the edge of a

wood, and follow it round to the right. Continue through a gate along the edge of a field and then along a track and a private road past Gostrode Farm. Just before the road swings right, take a path on the left and continue into a wood to rejoin the SBP. Turn right back to the start.

Note: The paths just north of the SBP for two kilometres east of Gostrode Farm present difficulties.

8. Alfold Bars to Honeywood House

Distance: SBP: 9.5 km, 6 miles. **Return:** 12 km, 7.5 miles.

Maps: Explorer 134, Landranger 186 and 187.

En route: *Rudgwick:* pub and shops.

Things to see: *Rudgwick:* Holy Trinity Church, XIV century.

You are almost as likely to see deer as sheep or cattle on this walk, which passes two deer farms. There are some good views to the Surrey hills and the South Downs. The return walk passes some splendid timber-framed buildings.

1. SBP: Follow Pigbush Lane (036333), opposite the Sir Roger Tichborne, to Keepers Cottage, where the metalled lane ends. Take a track along the edge of a wood and follow it round to the left. Just past a pond on the left turn right along a track. This brings you to a junction of six tracks, not all of which may appear on the map.

2. Continue in almost the same direction, along an earth track under trees. At the end of the wood follow a path through the grounds of Rikkyo School. Pass the car park and cross a junction of drives into a field. Bear left to the A281 by Lower Hill House.

3. Opposite the house take a lane signposted *Baynards* and *Cranleigh*. Cross another lane to a gate with a sign *Wellgrove Farm.* Take a path to the left of the gate and go through three narrow kissing gates, with a deer farm on the right. Continue along the edges of three fields, with good views north and south, to a mobile 'phone tower and a wood. Continue through the wood (the first part of which older maps may show as

open ground), where a brief detour to the left may be made to visit the trig point. The Downs Link Bridleway joins on the left, and soon after this the Footpath and Cycleway. Continue into a field, aiming for the end of a row of trees. Follow the edge of the next field above a clay pit, and in the next turn right and go through a wood. Cross a small field and turn right along a path to the B2128 at Rudgwick.

4. Turn right into the village and the Kings Head. If you continue south you will come to shops. Just past the pub, turn left and climb steps to Holy Trinity Church. Follow a path past the church and across a small field to a track. Turn left and immediately right past High Croft Cottage. Continue along the edge of a field and cross a track to a stile and a metalled track. At this point the map may show the SBP going north-east along a track (which is actually on the border) but the signpost correctly indicates a path going east across a field. Follow this path, and bear left along the edge of a wood to Hermongers.

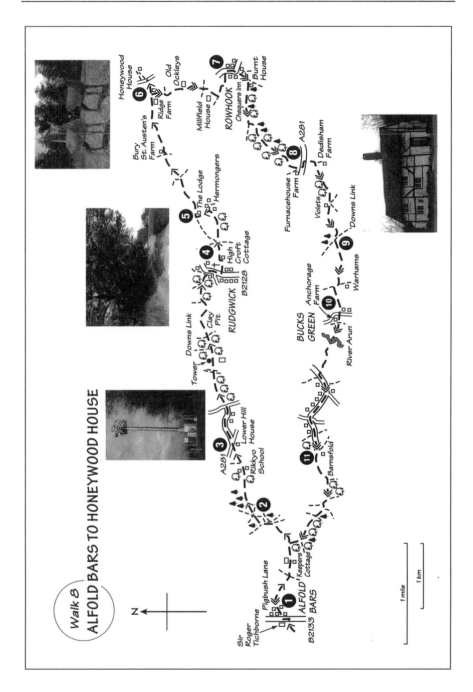

Walk 8
ALFOLD BARS TO HONEYWOOD HOUSE

N

1 mile
1 km

Sir Roger Tichborne
Plabush Lane
B2133 BARS
ALFOLD
Keepers Cottage

Rikkyo School
A281
Lower Hill House

Downs Link
Tower
Clay Pit
RUDGWICK
High Croft Cottage
B2128

The Lodge
Hermongers

Bury St. Austen's Farm
Ridge Farm
Honeywood House
Old Ockleys
Millfield House
ROWHOOK
Chequers Inn
Burnt House

Furnacehouse Farm
A281
Violets
Dedisham Farm
Downs Link
Warhams

BUCKS GREEN
Anchorage Farm
River Arun

Barnsfold

The SBP between Hermongers and Ridge Farm, near Rudgwick

Bear left along a drive between buildings and a bungalow. At a T-junction, turn left and follow the drive to The Lodge.

5. Immediately past the house, turn right along the edge of a field. Continue by a deer farm on the right to join a concrete track to Bury St. Austens Farm. Go through the farmyard and continue along a concrete track past Ridge Farm (there is another Ridge Farm on Walk 9) to the road at Honeywood House.

6. Return: Go back to Ridge Farm (it is assumed that you have conscientiously walked *all* of this section of the SBP). Go *past* the footpath sign (the route indicated was impassable in 1998) and turn left just past the first building. Go left and right to follow a grassy track along the edge of a field and through another field to a pond. Continue halfway along the edge of the next field, cross a stile and follow a narrow path beside the field. Continue along a grassy track and a private road until it swings right to Millfield House. Keep straight on along the left edge of a field and at its corner turn left. Go into the left-hand of two fields and follow its right edge. Go right and left along the edges of the next field to a road. Turn right to Rowhook and **The Chequers Inn**, where the old pillory may be seen.

7. Take a lane which goes uphill beside the inn. At the top turn right towards Burnt House and take a path on the right along the edge of a wood.

Where the path swings left to join another turn back left for a few paces, then turn right along a path which goes SW away from the edge of the wood. Two paths join from the left. Continue to a track, turn left and follow it to a metalled drive by Furnacehouse Farm, where the furnace served the glass industry. Turn left to the A281.

8. Turn left and shortly right along a concrete track to Dedisham Farm. Just before houses turn right along a track with a sign *Violets*. The river on the right is the Arun. A little before the beautiful old house fork left and walk through a gravelled yard to a small gate. Turn right and follow the edge of a field down into a dip by the corner of the hedge, then bear left across the field to a wood. Bear left across a footbridge, turn right beside the old railway embankment (which is part of the Downs Link) and then left to cross it.

9. Continue along the edge of a field. At its corner cross a footbridge on the right and follow the edge of a field with a tall hedge on the right. Bear right across a narrow field, continue along the edge of the next and then along a narrow path between wire fences to another narrow path below Warhams. Turn right and shortly left over a stile. Cross a field and continue along a path between a hedge and a fence to a road at Bucks Green.

10. Turn right and cross to the track to Anchorage Farm. Immediately cross a stile and follow a path along the edge of fields and over the River Arun. Continue along a track to a stile, turn left and bear right to follow

the left edge of a field to a road. Turn left along the road and then right along a lane signposted *Tisman's Common*. Continue over a cross-roads and at the end of the road continue along a track past Barnsfold.

11. The next section requires care. Enter a wood and fork right along its edge. Keep right at a junction. At the next junction keep left. At the next, by a small bridge, keep right. At the next, by a wooden fence, keep left and continue along the edge of the wood with fields on the right. Continue over a track with a sign *Pallinghurst Estate Murrayswood* to rejoin the SBP near Keepers Cottage. Turn left and walk back to Alfold Bars.

9. Honeywood House to The Royal Oak

Distance: SBP: 10 km, 6 miles. **Return:** 7 km, 4.5 miles.

Maps: Explorer 134, Landranger 187.

En route: *Kingsfold:* pub.

The walk goes through pleasant countryside, but there are few extensive views. The proximity of Gatwick Airport makes this and the following walks noisy. In the eastern section, metal bridle gates should be treated with care – it is surprisingly easy to mash a finger.

1. SBP: Take a path (120355) just to the left of the grounds of Honeywood House and follow it through a wood, where it broadens into a track and leads to a road. Turn back to the right along a metalled drive, go past Honeybush Farm to Monks Farm, and turn left at a T-junction.

2. You are now on Stane Street, an old Roman road. Continue through a small wood and uphill between fields. At the top turn right along a metalled drive. Follow this past a small wood until it turns right (this part may not appear on your map). Keep straight on between trees to the edge of a wood. Do not take the wooden gate directly ahead; go about 10 metres to the right to a similar gate and follow a path along the edge of a wood. Continue through the wood and between fields to the A29.

3. Cross and take a concrete track to Denne Farm. Go through the farm buildings and continue between fields. Where the track swings right, take a grassy path on the left. Continue through a small wood, cross a field to a gate and cross another field to the corner of Rowland Wood and a bridge. Follow the edge of the next field for a short distance round to the left, and go through a small wooden gate into the wood. Follow the path through the wood to join a track by the corner of a field. Turn left along the track and almost immediately right along another track through a strip of woodland. Continue to a lane at Payne's Green and turn right.

4. Just past a bridge over the North River take a concrete track on the right with signs to *Oakdale Farm* and *Upper Oakdale*. Follow the track past Oakdale Farm (do not take the left turn to the farm). At the next house (presumably Upper Oakdale) the concrete track ends. Continue along a grassy track between fields. Join another track by a pond on the left and continue uphill to a corrugated iron barn. Bear left along a track and follow it to Wattlehurst Farm.

5. Just past the farmhouse turn left along a grassy track and continue along the edge of a field. Go through a small wood and past a pond, and continue uphill by power lines. At the top of the hill turn left towards Bonnetts Farm. Go past a duckpond and through the farmyard. Just past double gates turn right along a track

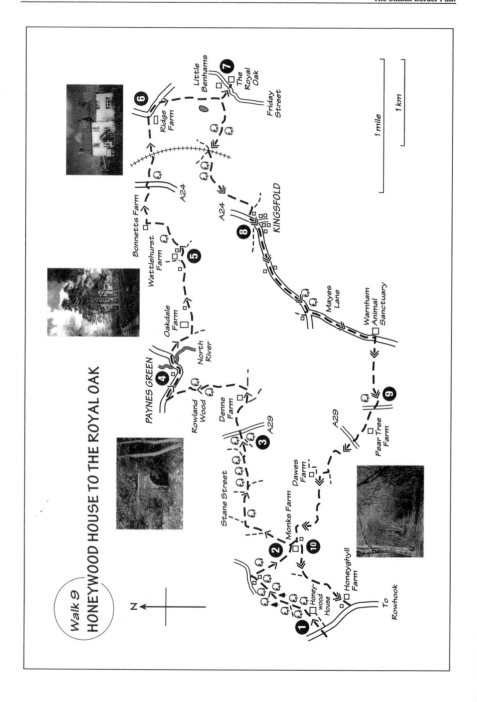

Walk 9
HONEYWOOD HOUSE TO THE ROYAL OAK

to the A24. Turn left and very shortly right into a field. Follow the edge of the field to cross a railway bridge and continue along the edge of the next field to the buildings of Ridge Farm (there is another Ridge Farm on Walk 8). Pass the farm buildings on the right and turn left along a track to a road.

6. Turn right and just over a bridge take a footpath on the right. Go diagonally across a field which shows signs of motorcycle racing, aiming first for a signpost and then for a stile. Cross the next field to a footbridge with two stiles, and continue to a similar combination in the corner of the next. There is a large pond on the right which may not appear on the map. Continue along the edge of the next field, and in the next bear right to a signpost and footbridge. Do not cross the footbridge; turn left along the edge of the field and continue through the next, past Little Benhams, to a lane and **The Royal Oak**. Try the bubble.

7. Return: Follow the SBP back to the first footbridge. This time cross it and turn right. Walk into the next field and turn left along its edge. At the far end turn left into a strip of woodland, cross a footbridge and continue along the edge of a field towards a railway. Turn right and then left to cross the lines, and take the left-hand of two paths diagonally across a field. Continue beside a wood which contains an old moat. Cross a strip of woodland into a field and bear left to its far corner. Cross a stile (not the gate on the right) and follow the right edges of two fields.

Turn right over a stile and follow a path towards houses and the A24 at Kingsfold.

8. Turn left and then right by the Wise Old Owl, along the road to Billingshurst. Turn left along Mayes Lane, and follow it to Warnham Animal Sanctuary. Take a path opposite along the edge of a field. Cross a strip of woodland and a small field and cross a larger field to the edge of a wood. Continue with the wood on the right, then go through a strip of woodland and along the edge of a field to a road.

9. Turn right and left along a private road to Pear Tree Farm. Walk past the farm to the A29, cross and continue along a path. Bear left and right over footbridges, continue to the corner of a field and turn right to Dawes Farm. At the buildings, turn left along a concrete track and go gently uphill. At the top, follow the track round two bends to the right. Go slightly downhill and round to the left, and continue to Monks Farm (where it is possible to join the outward route).

10. Just past the first building, a stable block, take a path on the left along the edge of a field and turn right just before a metal gate. Follow a path which winds between fences and hedges to the corner of a wood and bear left into the wood. The paths here are faint but the route is well sign-posted. Just before a small stream turn left, cross a footbridge on the right and continue to a track. Turn left and follow the track through woodland and fields to the road by Honeyghyll Farm. Turn right and walk back to the start.

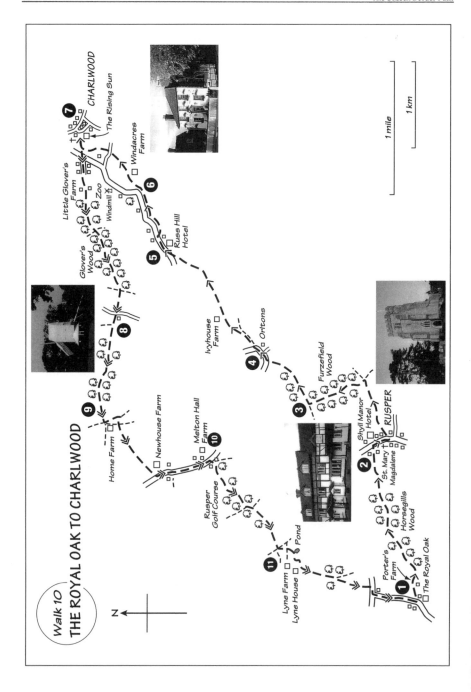

Walk 10
THE ROYAL OAK TO CHARLWOOD

N

Home Farm
Newhouse Farm
Melton Hall Farm
Rusper Golf Course
Lyne Farm
Lyne House
Pond
Porter's Farm
Horsegills Wood
The Royal Oak
St. Mary Magdalene
RUSPER
Shyll Manor Hotel
Furzefield Wood
Ohtons
Ivyhouse Farm
Rues Hill Hotel
Glover's Wood
Little Glover's Farm
Zoo
Windmill
Windacres Farm
The Rising Sun
CHARLWOOD

1 mile
1 km

10. The Royal Oak to Charlwood

Distance: SBP: 8 km, 5 miles. **Return:** 9 km, 5.5 miles.

Maps: Explorer 134 and 146, Landranger 187.

En route: *Rusper:* pub and shops. *Gatwick Zoo:* café.

Parking: by the Royal Oak, or on the road to the south.

Things to see: *Rusper:* Church of St Mary Magdalene; Ghyll Manor: timber-framed house, now hotel. *Charlwood:* Gatwick Zoo: daily from 1030, tel: 01293 826312 (no pets); Lowfield Heath Windmill: (by zoo), exterior at any time, interior some Sunday afternoons, tel: 01293 862646; Church of St. Nicholas: XI century.

This walk offers a pleasant blend of farmland and woodland. Although not hilly, there are good views. Large hotels indicate the proximity of Gatwick Airport.

---

1. SBP: From the Royal Oak (184368), turn right and walk north. Just past Howell's Gill, cross a footbridge on the right. Follow the edge of a small field and bear left across the next to the end of a wooden fence. Turn right along a track, and almost immediately left to a gate under a tree. Follow the edge of a field with Porter's Farm on the right and cross a stile on the right. Turn left and follow the path into Horsegill's Wood. Turn left along a path and almost at once take a path on the right beside a stream. Follow the stream through the wood until the path swings left into a field. Follow the edge of the field until, just before its end, a stile leads back into the wood. Turn left along a path and descend a steep gully to the second of two footbridges. Keep right up the hill and turn left at the top. Leave the wood and continue along the edge of a field and a sports field to the road at Rusper.

2. Turn right past the Ghyll Manor Hotel (a fine building – peep through the gate), the Plough Inn and the Church of St Mary Magdalene. If you continue into the village you will find the village stores and another pub, The Star. Turn left just past a car showroom. Follow a path gently downhill along the left-hand edge of a field, then take a path between a hedge and a fence into another field. Continue past an isolated strip of hedge to a row of tall trees and turn left. Follow a path along the edge of a field into Furzefield Wood. Cross a footbridge and continue along the edges of two fields with the wood on your left. Continue through the wood to a point near the corner of a field and turn right.

3. Shortly leave the wood and continue along the edge of a field. Enter another wood, and follow its edge round to the left into a field with a large white house (Orltons) ahead. Cross the field to a lane and turn right.

4. Continue past a lane on the right. Where the road swings left, cross a stile on the right and follow the edge of a field parallel to a concrete track. There are good views to the North Downs on the left and the buildings of Gatwick Airport come into view ahead. Where the track swings right, bear slightly left across the field, aiming for a red house to the left of farm buildings. At the end of a hedge, turn right and continue past Ivyhouse Farm with the hedge on your left. Continue across the next field, aiming to the right of a clump of small trees which grow in a pond. At the pond bear left to the corner of the field, where there is a prominent post. Follow the edge of the next field for a short distance and bear left to its opposite corner and a road.

5. Turn right past the Russ Hill Hotel. Just past the hotel sign, which hangs from an oak, cross a stile and walk along the edge of a field parallel to the road. Return to the road briefly past Russ Hill House and then rejoin the path. There is a good view over the airport from this point. Continue through two fields to a point where the road swings left. A detour can be made along the road to visit Gatwick Zoo and Lowfield Heath Windmill.

6. Take a path which runs parallel to the track leading to Windacre (Windacres?) Farm. The windmill appears on the left – some way from Lowfield Heath, having been dismantled and moved. Follow the path past the farm buildings and continue to the left-hand corner of a field. Bear left across the next field to its opposite corner. Cross another path into a field and follow a path through a gap in a hedge. Bear left to a stile in the left-hand corner of a field. Continue along the edge of a field to a stile and then along the edge of another field. Cross a farm bridge, and bear right to a stile by the church. Turn right

The Rising Sun, Charlwood

along a path through the churchyard into **Charlwood**. Turn right into a road by the Half Moon pub. In the village there are two more pubs, The Rising Sun and the Greyhound, the Pine Cafe, the Limes Bistro and shops.

7. Return: Follow the path back through the churchyard and keep straight on. Cross a road and continue along Glover's Road, which is public, to the private road to Little Glover's Farm. Continue along a path into Glover's Wood, which is a nature reserve worth detailed exploration. Follow a waymarked path through the wood over several crossing paths and a footbridge. Continue between fields to a road.

8. Turn right and immediately left by a wooden fence and cross a field, bearing slightly left to a strip of woodland. Cross this and bear right along the edge of a field, with the wood on your right. At the end of the field continue into the wood. Bear right over a footbridge and a stile, and then bear left along the edge of a field. Re-enter the wood and cross a footbridge. Bear right and then left over another footbridge. Cross two fields towards the buildings of Home Farm.

9. By the farm, turn left and take the left-hand of two tracks. Follow it past the farm buildings and turn right through a metal gate. Cross a field and continue along the right edge of the next two fields. Bear a little away from the edge of the next and in the next bear left to a track beside Newhouse Farm. Turn left along a road and continue past Rusper Golf Club.

10. Just past Melton Hall Farm cross a stile on the right and turn left. Turn right behind stables and continue along the edges of three fields, with a wood on your left. Cross a stile and bear right across the golf course to a hedge. Keep this on your left and continue into a strip of woodland. Cross a footbridge and bear left across the golf course into woodland. Follow a track through trees and grassy clearings and turn left at a T-junction of tracks. Where the track swings left cross a stile and bear right across a field to the left of a clump of trees which contains a pond. Bear right along the edge of a field and cross the next towards the buildings of Lyne Farm.

11. Cross a track and bear left across a field, to the middle of its far side (the small wood which may appear on your map no longer exists). Cross the track which leads to the farm, continue to a pond and bear right towards Lyne House. Follow a track round to the right below the grounds and then bear left downhill beside a row of trees and fence posts into a wood. Cross a footbridge and bear right uphill. At the top bear right along a faint path, and cross a footbridge to the corner of a field. Cross the field bearing slightly away from its left side and cross the next field to a road. Turn right and then left at a signpost *Langhurst*, and follow the lane back to the Royal Oak.

11. Charlwood to Copthorne

Distance: SBP: 11 km, 7 miles. **Return:** 12 km, 7.5 miles.

Maps: Explorer 146, 135 (18), 134 (for return only), Landranger 187.

En route: *Hookwood:* hotels. *Gatwick Airport:* hotels. *Horley:* pub. *Tinsley Green:* (on return) pub.

Things to see: G*atwick Airport. Burstow:* Church of St Bartholomew*:* XII century, timber tower.

I should find it difficult to say which part of the SBP I like best, but I have no doubt about the one I like least. The section which skirts Gatwick Airport is noisy, smelly, litter-strewn and complicated. Its only merit is its brevity. A more pleasant alternative is recommended. The return south of the airport is also marred by industrial estates. There are no extensive views.

---

1. SBP From the Half Moon (241410) walk east along the main road towards Gatwick, and turn left along Chapel Road. At the end of the road, continue along a track into open country. At a T-junction of tracks turn right and follow a path along the edge of a field. At another junction of tracks continue through fields towards red houses and turn left along a road.

2. Continue to a track on the right with signs *GAL Property Keep Out* (1998 – development may take place here). Follow a path beside the road, turn right through a strip of woodland and then go along the edge of a wood. At the corner of a field turn left, cross a footbridge and turn left again along a track. At a T-junction of tracks turn right and continue towards the perimeter of the airport. Turn left along a pleasant path which winds beside the River Mole, and go under a road bridge. About 300 metres further on, where there is a wider area of grass, the alternative route begins – see below. For the official route, continue past the Ramada hotel. Cross a footbridge and bear right along a path beside the A23 (not the more obvious path beside the river). It is not possible to cross the A23 at this point.

3. The next section is intricate and needs care. There are numerous signs, some of them special ones with black initials W.S.B.P. and a walker logo on a yellow background, as well as conventional wooden and metal signposts, but they can be difficult to spot. At a roundabout cross two roads towards le Meridien hotel. Do not cross the next road (Crossway); turn left along the pavement and then cross the road to a point under the elevated railway. Turn left and follow a tarmac path with the railway on your right. At a road (Gatwick Way) turn right under

Horses near railway, Gatwick

the railway to a T-junction, and turn left to cross the road. You are now on Perimeter Road North. Walk behind the Police Station and beside the railway to a roundabout. Turn left to follow a pedestrian way through a tunnel, and turn left through another tunnel. At the exit from this turn right and go under the elevated railway. Go through a third tunnel and turn left along a path beside the railway, which is the London-Brighton line. Fences and locked gates leave no choices about the route until a footbridge on the right.

The alternative: Take a path on the left to a road. Turn right, walk to a roundabout and cross the A23. Turn right and just past a bridge over the Gatwick Stream, take a path on the

left. Turn right and follow a path through Riverside Garden Park between the A23 and the stream. At a fork bear left and cross a road bridge. Turn right along a road and at its end take a path on the left. Turn right along The Crescent and just before its end turn left. Take a path to the left of number 114, which leads to the railway footbridge and the official route.

4. Cross the footbridge and follow a path leading away from the railway. Follow the path towards a group of white houses, bearing right and then left across a field and beside houses to the B2036. Turn right past the Coppingham Arms pub. Just before the M23 (spur) bridge turn left along a path beside a tarmac drive. Con-

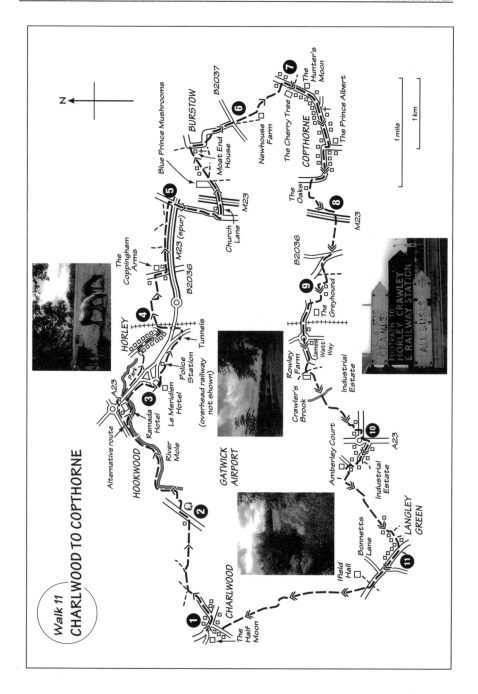

Walk 11
CHARLWOOD TO COPTHORNE

tinue beside the motorway and join a track which leads to a road.

5. Turn right, go under the motorway and continue past a Z-bend. Take Church Lane on the left; this is a public road although it may appear as a bridleway on your map. Follow the lane over the M23 to the Blue Prince Mushrooms complex, and keep straight on along a track. Follow this round to the left and continue past houses, woodland and an old moat to a lane at Moat End House, Burstow. Turn right past the Church of St. Bartholomew. Where the lane turns left there are two footpaths. Take the one on the left and make for the far corner of a field, where a stile may be difficult to find in summer foliage, and rejoin the lane. Turn right, continue to the B2037 (Antlands Lane) and cross it.

6. At the beginning of the drive to Newhouse Farm, cross a stile on the left and cross a field, aiming to the left of the farm buildings. Cross a footbridge by the farm, turn left along a concrete track and follow it round to the right. Cross the corner of a field and cross another field, aiming to the right of a white house. Turn right along a road to **Copthorne** and The Cherry Tree.

7. Return: Continue south into Copthorne which, now a quiet dormitory village, was once famous for two violent activities – smuggling and prize-fighting. Pass the Hunter's Moon Inn (accommodation) and follow the road round to the right past the Church of St. John The Evangelist and shops. Turn right at a T-junction by The Prince Albert and

follow the road round to the left and then to the right. Just before a drive with a sign *The Oaks* take a path on the left. Follow the edge of a field to its corner, turn left and about two-thirds of the way along cross a footbridge on the right and walk to the M23. Turn left beside the motorway and then right to cross it.

8. Follow a made path to the B2036. Cross and take a road signposted *Gatwick* and *Manor Royal*. At a drive on the left with a sign *Forge Wood* take a path which crosses the drive diagonally. Follow the left edge of a field to its corner, turn right and continue past a house on the left to a metalled drive. Turn left and follow the drive through the yard of W.H. Maslen. Cross a bridge, go through a wide metal gate, and shortly turn right at a gap and follow the edges of two fields to a road.

9. Turn left past The Greyhound and cross the railway to a roundabout. The next section was being developed in 1998 and may have changed. Cross the roundabout and continue along James Watt Way, a road which may appear as a bridleway on your map. Where the road swings left, continue along a track to Rowley Farm. At a double gate just before the farm turn left along a track into a field. Bear right along its edge for a short distance and then cross to a footbridge over Crawler's Brook in the opposite corner. Continue across the next field to a row of trees. Bear left along the edge of a field towards an industrial estate and just before the buildings bear right across the corner of a field. Zigzag left and right

Village sign, Charlwood

and turn left between industrial buildings to a road. Turn right to a roundabout and turn left along the A23.

10. Cross the A23 and just before a filling station turn right and continue along a road (County Oak Way) through the industrial estate. At Whitworth Road take a track between buildings and follow it round to the right to the car park at Amberley Court. Turn left along the edge of the car park and cross a stile into a field. Turn left into the next field and then right along its edge. At the corner turn left and follow the edge for about three-quarters of its length to a gap (not the first) in the hedge. Bear right across the corner of a field to a footbridge and stile. Almost immediately cross another stile on the right. Cross a narrow field and continue

over another stile and a concrete bridge. Turn left over a stile and follow the right edge of a long field. Continue past a caravan site to a drive. Follow it round to the left and turn right along a path and a track to a road and the houses of Langley Green. Follow a minor road for a short distance and continue along a path between houses.

11. At the main road turn right and follow it past two junctions to the drive to Ifield Hall. Just past here, take a footpath on the right which runs, for two-and-a-half kilometres, back to Charlwood. Turn right and follow a road into the village.

12. Copthorne to East Grinstead

Distance: SBP: 11.5 km, 7 miles. **Return:** 9 km, 5.5 miles.

Maps: Explorer 135 (18), Landranger 187.

En route: *Crawley Down:* pub and shops.

Things to see: *Crawley Down:* Rowfant House: not open to the public. *East Grinstead:* High Street: many fine buildings from XIV to XIX centuries; Sackville College: Jacobean almshouses, Jun-Aug, Weds to Suns, 1400-1700, tel: 01342 321930; Church of St. Swithun; Town Trails: old and new; Town Museum: Weds and Sats 1400-1600. Gullege: old house with fine Jacobean frontage, not open to the public.

This walk follows a variety of paths, tracks, private roads and an old railway. It goes through the grounds of a famous building, Rowfant House, and finishes at East Grinstead, where the Mid-Sussex Link leaves for the south. The walking is easy, but lacks extensive views.

1. SBP: From the Cherry Tree (321399) turn right, walk south for a short distance and turn left along Clay Hall Lane. Where the metalled section ends, turn right through a gate with a sign *Roundabouts Farm*. Follow a track past the house, which may not appear on the map. Where the track swings to the left past the house, keep straight on through a metal kissing gate, which for once has room for the largest rucksack. Follow a path round to the left behind houses and continue along a track. Follow this round to the right to the A264 by The Abergavenny Arms.

2. Cross the road, and take a metalled track through Copthorne Common. At a junction of tracks turn slightly to the left following a sign *Hunter's Lodge Fishery*. Follow the track in almost a straight line through fields and woodland. Locked gates and *Pri-*

vate signs make it unlikely that you will go astray. Just past Keeper's Cottage, where the metalled track swings left, keep straight on along a track. When this in turn swings left, continue along a path and then a track past Home Farm. Where the main track turns left by Hill House, keep straight on along a path which goes downhill and to the right. Cross a stream, turn right along a track behind Rowfant House, and then left through an arch. The way through the grounds is well signposted. The house, supposed to have been built in the Elizabethan period for an iron-master, now belongs to a charitable foreign organisation. Follow the drive round to the left and take a path on the right. Follow this over a stone bridge and through the grounds of a bungalow to a road.

3. Turn left and just after Fern Cottage turn right along a drive, by a sign

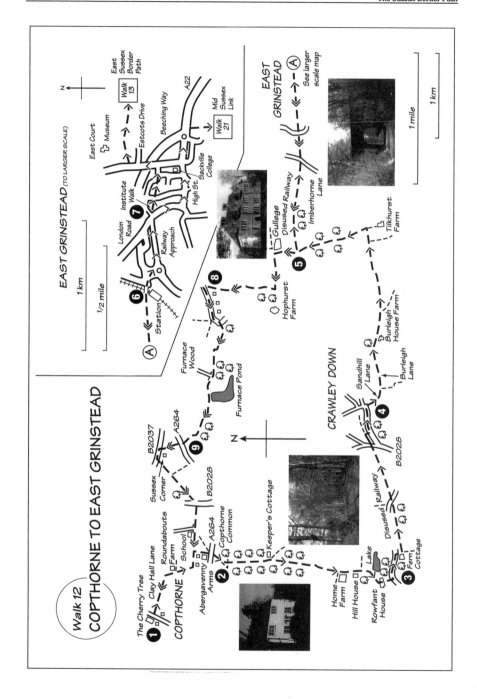

Walk 12
COPTHORNE TO EAST GRINSTEAD

Rowfant Business School. Almost at once, take a path on the left leading to an old railway line. This section of the SBP is shared by the Worth Way. Follow the old line for one-and-a-half kilometres, going over a lane and under a bridge bearing the B2028. A little further on, at the top of a short rise, take steps going uphill to the right and follow a path to Grange Road. You are now in Crawley Down, which is mainly a modern development. Turn left, and follow the road until it swings left. If you continue along the road, you will come almost at once to a small shopping centre, the village green and The Royal Oak.

4. Turn right along Sandhill Lane, a private road, and follow it uphill and to the left. Where Sandhill Lane turns right, keep straight on along Burleigh Lane. Go to the left of Burleigh House Farm, follow a path along the edge of a field and go straight across the next. Cross a footbridge and continue along the short edge of a field to a stile with a stream on the left. In the next field continue beside the stream to the corner of a wood and then keep straight on across a field. Keep straight on through a gap in the hedge, and cross the next field to a stile. In a small field, with the buildings of Tilkhurst Farm a little way to the right, turn left along a grassy track through a field. In the next field, where the track swings away to the right, take a path leading across the field to the left of a clump of trees, which conceals a pond. Cross another field to a clump

of bushes. Follow the path to the left through a metal kissing gate and back onto the old railway line.

5. This section is shared by the Worth Way and a High Weald Circular Walk. Turn right and walk towards East Grinstead, passing under two high road bridges. You are now in the suburbs of East Grinstead, but the wooded sides of the cutting give a rural air for a little longer. The track leads to the car park at East Grinstead Railway Station. Follow the track beside the car park, cross its corner, and cross the railway by a footbridge. Follow a stepped path round to the right to East Grinstead Station, where there is another car park and a Sainsbury's supermarket.

East Grinstead is the largest town traversed by the SBP. Although it is mainly modern, its growth promoted by the construction of the railway to London in the XIX century, it has in its High Street a magnificent collection of old buildings.

6. Turn left and walk beside the car park to a road interchange. Cross to Railway Approach, on the right of the Mid-Sussex Timber Building. Continue to London Road and turn right. At traffic lights, the two branches of the SBP separate. For the East Sussex section, see Walk 13, for the Mid-Sussex Link, Walk 21.

7. **Return:** Retrace your steps along the old railway for just over 2km. to a junction south of Gullege. Turn right and continue past the house, which is well seen from this approach. Turn left and follow a track to the corner of a wood. Fork right and follow a path with the wood on the left. Turn right

between fields and continue across another field, in which there are traces of a mediaeval village, best seen from the track below. Turn left along the track and follow it to a road.

8. Turn left and follow the road to a bend to the left, just before which a path on the right should be ignored. Go round the bend, and take a path on the right through uncultivated ground. Continue across a field, turn right between houses and left along a private road. Where this turns right by *Furnace*, keep straight on along a path. Cross the dam of Furnace Pond, below which there are traces of the old iron workings. Continue uphill to a field; follow its edge for about 40 metres and take a stile on the right, which is easily missed, between holly bushes. Cross a field to the cor-

ner of a wood and continue with the wood on the left. Follow a path through the wood and at its edge turn right. Continue past buildings and along a drive to the A264.

9. Cross and continue along a path and then a track. By the garage of Rossley, bear left along a drive and follow it to the B2037.Turn left and take the first track on the left by *Sussex Corner* (a house). Continue to the B2028. Cross and follow Mill Lane to Copthorne School. By the school gates take a path on the left and follow it round to the right, keeping as close as possible to the school grounds. At the end of the school buildings, turn left and continue beside an old ditch and embankment. Rejoin the SBP by houses and follow it back to the start.

Gullege: Jacobean ironmaster's house

East Sussex

Converted oast at Quedley, near Union Street (Walk 18)

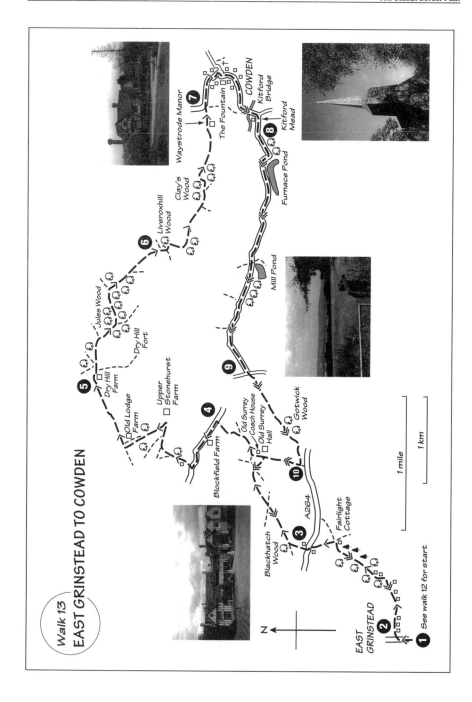

Walk 13
EAST GRINSTEAD TO COWDEN

13. East Grinstead to Cowden

Distance: SBP: 12 km, 7.5 miles. **Return:** 9 km, 5.5 miles.

Maps: Explorer 135 (18) and 147, Landranger 187 and 188.

Parking: Estcots Drive, East Court area.

Things to see: *Old Surrey Hall; Waystrode Manor:* timber-framed mansions, neither open to the public.

This walk passes several fine old buildings, including the two above. The views are excellent. In Spring, woods are carpeted with bluebells, and fields and gardens with daffodils. The lane used for part of the return has little traffic and lots of interest.

1.SBP: From the traffic lights (393381) in East Grinstead, follow Institute Walk to the right of a car showroom. Cross a road and continue along another walk, past a car park and along De La Warr Road. At its end, turn left and cross a bridge over Beeching Way, an old railway cutting converted to a road. It is named, perhaps ironically, after Richard Beeching, who closed much of the rail network in the 1960s, but not the line to East Grinstead where he lived. Cross Estcots Drive, and continue to the entrance to East Court, a pleasant piece of parkland containing several municipal buildings, including the Town Museum.

2. Turn right down a private road and continue along a footpath. Pass a playing field and continue with houses on the right. Cross a footbridge and continue through woodland to a private road by Fairlight Cottage. Turn left to the A264.

3. Turn left and almost immediately right along a path which is not obvious. Go downhill over a landfill site

to Blackhatch Wood. A short distance into the wood, turn right over a footbridge and cross a field to its opposite corner. Cross a track to the corner of another field and cross this diagonally to a gate. Continue along a track through woodland to Old Surrey Hall. Turn left along a gravelled drive to the left of Old Surrey Coach House and follow a path through the garden. Turn left uphill along a track and, where it swings left, take a path on the right by holly trees. Continue between fields to a road.

4. Turn left along the road past Blockfield Farm to a sign *Bidbury.* Turn right and follow a track between wooden fences. Pass a barn and stables, and continue along a path to a grassy ride between wooden fences, which may not be shown on the Explorer map. Where the ride swings left cross a stile on the right and cross a field. Turn right along a metalled drive. At the bottom of a dip cross a stile on the left and follow the edge of the field to a stile on the right. Continue uphill, keep-

The Sussex Border Path near Dormansland

ing to the left of a hedge, to Old Lodge Farm. Go between the farm buildings and turn right along a private road. Continue past Dry Hill Farm (where a short diversion south can be made to visit Dry Hill Fort) and along a track through woodland.

5. Continue past an orchard on the left into Jules Wood, and follow the path round to the right. Just after a slight descent take a path on the left which goes downhill. Leave the wood and follow the edge of a field round to the right and back into the wood at a metal gate. Follow a path through the wood and then along its edge. At a gate, cross a field to its opposite corner and continue along the edge of the next field. At a junction of paths cross a track and take a path into Liveroxhill Wood.

6. Walk past a pond into a field, and turn right and then left along its edges. Pass a gate on the right, and at the next gate cross a stile. Continue downhill along the edge of a field to a stile on the left. Follow the right edge of the next field, and in the next go past a derelict barn and follow its left edge, bearing left into Clay's Wood. Walk through the wood, turn right and cross a field diagonally. The spire of the church at Cowden appears ahead. Bear slightly left across the next field and cross a footbridge into a wood. Continue uphill, turning right when the path joins another, to Waystrode Manor. Continue along the drive to a road.

7. Continue along the road into Cowden. At a road junction turn left to continue the SBP, or right to **The Fountain**, an old-style village pub.

8. Return: from The Fountain, continue south and east along the road to Kitford Bridge. Just past Kitford Mead, turn right along a lane and follow it for over three kilometres.

9. At a T-junction, turn left and then right over a stile. Follow the top edge of a field and cross the middle of the next, ignoring the more obvious path along its top. Go through a strip of woodland and cross a field to its bottom corner. Cross a footbridge and climb through uncultivated ground to a field. Follow a row of trees, cross a track (which may not appear on the map) and skirt the edge of Gotwick Wood. Re-cross the track and cross a field, moving uphill to rejoin the track. Follow the track to a private road and turn right.

10. Walk to Old Surrey Hall, and turn left to follow the SBP back to East Grinstead.

14. Cowden to Groombridge

Distance: SBP: 10.5 km, 6.5 miles. **Return:** 10 km, 6 miles.

Maps: Explorer 147 & 135 (18), Landranger 188.

En route: *Ashurst* pub.

Things to see: *Groombridge Place Gardens:* formal gardens, enchanted forest, parkland, Good Friday to 25 Oct, 1000 -1800, tel: 01892 863999.

Streams and railways, used and disused, feature prominently in this walk. The streams are crossed and re-crossed, and care is needed to avoid finding yourself on the wrong side. The only hilly section is south of Ashurst, where the best views are seen before the SBP descends to the River Medway. The 'Pond Bays' on this and other walks are relics of the Sussex iron industry, which depended on water power from artificial ponds. A 'bay' is a dam.

---

1. SBP: Walk down Church Street (465404) beside the Church of St. Mary Magdalene. At its end turn right and follow a grassy track downhill through allotments. Cross a lane and continue downhill beside a field. Walk along the edge of a golf course, cross a stream, and turn left. Follow a grassy path over the golf course, halfway between the stream and a wood. Cross a stile half-hidden in a hedge and continue across a field, aiming for a white gate. Continue to a stile below Sussex House Farm, and turn left to cross the stream by a farm bridge. Bear right away from the stream and follow a path beside the hedge. In the next field, continue beside the stream to the B2026 at Kentwater Cottages.

2. Turn right, cross a road bridge, then turn left and cross a series of stiles. Go through a metal gate and cross the stream by a footbridge.

Turn right and continue through fields with the stream on your right. There is a pond on the right, which may not appear on the map. Below Moat Farm cross a bridge and turn left and right without crossing a second, identical bridge. Continue through fields with the stream on your left, and two more ponds on the right, which may not appear on the map. Continue with a hedge on your left and turn left under a railway bridge. Turn half-right and cross a field towards a bend in the stream. Follow the path into the corner of the field and cross a stile, ignoring a bridge on the left. Cross the corner of the next field and turn left over a footbridge. Turn right and continue with the stream now on the right. The short-legged will not like the metal bridges on the next stretch. Continue beside the stream to join a lane below Hobbs Hill Farm.

SBP beside new-mown hay below Willetts Farm, near Ashurst

3. Turn right and almost immediately left over a stile, keeping the stream on your right. Follow the stream through fields with a golf course on the right. Cross a corner of the golf course and continue beside the stream through a field. Bear right along the edge of the next field.

4. At this point the SBP changes direction from east to south. At the corner of the field cross the stream by a footbridge and head uphill towards Willett's Farm. Follow the track through the farm with most of the buildings on your left. Dairy ice cream is on sale here in the Summer.

5. The next bit is tricky and not adequately waymarked (1998). Just past the farm the track swings right. Turn left to a large gap in a hedge with posts on each side. Do not go through the gap, but turn right and walk a short distance with the hedge on your left. At the corner of the hedge bear left through the middle of a field. Pass a pond on the right and another on the left and continue downhill through the middle of the field. Go through a narrow section of the field, and bear right below a wood. You are now beside the River Medway. Continue between the river and a small wood, then cross a field to its far corner below a railway embankment. Follow a path between the railway and the river, then go round to the right and under the railway. Continue along the edge of a field to the A264 (make a mental note of this point for the return). Turn left towards Ashurst.

6. Go over the river and under the railway. Just before The Bald Faced Stag, turn right along a road to Ashurst Station. Walk to the station and continue along a private road which swings away from the rail-

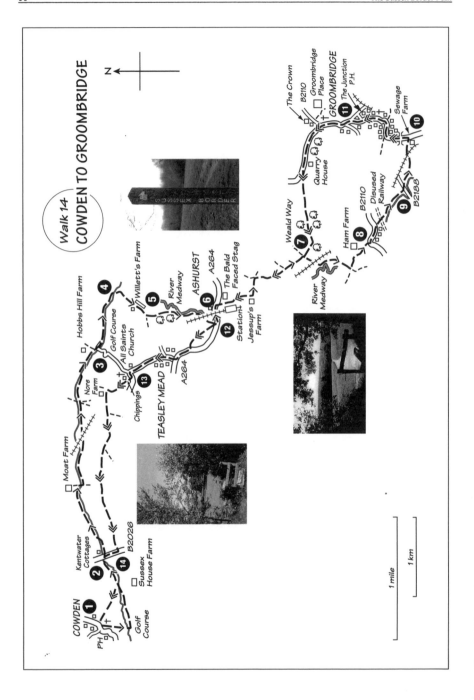

Walk 14
COWDEN TO GROOMBRIDGE

N

way. At the top of the hill, continue along the track past a large house, Linkhorns, which has a perilously leaning chimney. At Jessup's Farm, turn left uphill along a track. At the top turn right along a track and follow it downhill into a field past old farm buildings.

7. In the next field, turn right downhill towards the railway. This section of the SBP is shared by the Wealdway. Go under the railway, and turn left along a path leading away from the railway towards a footbridge (the Dick Taylor Memorial Bridge) by a clump of trees. You are now walking beside the Medway again. Bear right across the field to a bridge. Do not cross but turn left along a track towards Ham (Hamm?) Farm. Continue past the house to the B2110.

8. Turn left along the road. Just past a garage, cross a stile on the right into a field, and cross its corner to a disused railway. Cross this, turn left and walk away from the railway at a fine angle towards a bend in a stream. Follow the stream to the B2188.

9. Turn left and, just past a patch of woodland on the right, turn right into a field. Follow a faint path which bears left to meet a railway about three-quarters of the way along its edge. Go under the railway and turn right. Cross a field and follow a path to a road by a sewage farm.

10. Return: Turn left and follow the lane right and left into Groombridge, past a school and the Church of St. Thomas the Apostle. Turn right along Springfield Road to **The Junction**, which has railway memorabilia

in its bars. Nearby is the old station, converted into offices and a home. If you turn left by the pub you will come to shops, including a village stores and a bakery.

11. Continue to the B2110 and follow it past the entrance to Groombridge Place. Fork left along Bird-In-Hand Street (there is another pub, The Crown, a little further along the B2110). Just past Quarry House, take a footpath on the left and follow it through a field, across a lane and through a wood. Cross a field into another wood and cross a track. Cross two more fields to rejoin the SBP by Pond Wood. Retrace your route along the SBP until it leaves the A264 after Ashurst Bridge.

12. Turn right into a field and take the left-hand path, which first follows the hedge and then crosses the field to its top corner. Continue between trees to rejoin the A264, and follow it to Teasley Mead. Turn right along a lane and keep left at a fork. At the next junction, by All Saints Church, turn left.

13. Just past Chippings take a track on the right. Turn left just before Nore Farm, and follow the bridleway which runs just south of and above the SBP. This changes from path to track to metalled lane and meets the B2026.

14. Turn right to rejoin the SBP at Kentwater Cottages. Turn left and follow the SBP to the bridge below Sussex House Farm, but do not cross. Continue beside the stream to a concrete farm bridge. Cross this and bear right uphill along the side of a field back to Cowden.

15. Groombridge to Eridge Old Park

Distance: SBP: 10 km, 6 miles. **Return:** 11 km, 7miles. **Frant:** 1 km, 0.5 miles

Maps: Explorer 135 (18), Landranger 188.

En route: *Boarshead:* pub. *Eridge:* (on return) pub.

This is the first section of the SBP that I walked, and it is one of the best. It begins with a delightful little valley, and then goes through rolling countryside with a perfect mixture of fields and woods, and extensive views. The return along the High Weald Walk is almost as good. As a bonus, the walk passes many of the better-known sandstone outcrops in SE England.

Note: there are two Rocks Farms on this walk – one in section 2 and another in section 3.

1. SBP: Walk past the sewage farm (528365) and take a path on the right. Go under a railway and take a path on the left across a field. Descend to Motsmill Stream, and bear right along its bank through a narrow field and into a wood. Fork left to continue beside the stream. At Mott's Mill, continue uphill along a road.

2. Just past Meadowside, take a path on the left and descend to a footbridge. Continue uphill with Rock's Wood on the left. At the top of the steep part continue across a track, then go more gently uphill through fields, following power lines. By Bullfinches, at the top of the hill, the power lines go off to the left, and views open out. Continue downhill past a tennis court. At the bottom cross a footbridge and a track and continue uphill with a wood on your right. At the corner of the wood, bear right towards a clump of trees. Bear slightly left past the clump, and con-

tinue past a smaller clump on the left. Bear right to cross the next field diagonally, aiming for the corner of a large wood. Bear left over a farm bridge, and continue uphill along a sunken track. Turn right at a T-junction of tracks, and continue uphill along a track and then a sunken path. Join a track and continue past Renby Grange to the A26.

3. Cross to the end of an old road (which leads to the Boars Head Inn). Take a concrete track on the left and follow it round to the right past a high stone wall.

Note: In 1998 the SBP was due to be diverted here. The diversion goes downhill to the left along an avenue of lime trees, turns right along the bottom of a field and goes uphill to join the original route – see map.

Continue through Rocks Farm, and turn left and right to follow a track along the crest of a ridge (not the path *below* the ridge which may be shown on the map). Bowles Outdoor Pursuits Centre can be seen on the left, and the tower on Saxonbury Hill is prominent ahead. Follow the track round to the left and then to the right above the Centre, and continue along the bottom of a field. Bowles Rocks, a popular climbing area, is seen on the left. Continue downhill and cross a lane.

4. Continue downhill with Roughets Wood on the right. Cross a stile concealed in the corner of a field and continue over a farm bridge. Bear right to go under a railway bridge. Cross to the edge of a field and follow it uphill and round to the left. At the top, by a large oak tree, turn right to Stitches Farm. Follow a concrete track for a short distance, and just past the buildings turn left along a grassy track. Turn right before the next hedge and continue along the side of a field. Cross the first part of the next field to a corner and continue beside the hedge. Cross another field, and bear slightly left along the side of the next. At its corner turn right with a tall holly hedge on your left and continue to a road by Stonewall, a converted oast.

5. Turn right and then left down a lane, with fine views to the north. Just before Great Danegate turn left and follow a path downhill. Bear right into a wood and keep right at a fork. A short diversion to the left will lead you to two

odd towers with views over Eridge Old Park. Follow the path down through the wood to a gate in a deer fence (a very wet area), and bear right across a footbridge. Cross a track and follow a path which rises gently beside a stream. The path crosses the stream and climbs among trees and bracken until it swings left by a magnificent beech to re-cross the stream and reach open parkland. Fallow deer may be seen in the park; your chances of doing so will be greatly increased if any children in the party are securely gagged. Ignore a path going on up the hill, and turn right to

Stonewall: converted oast

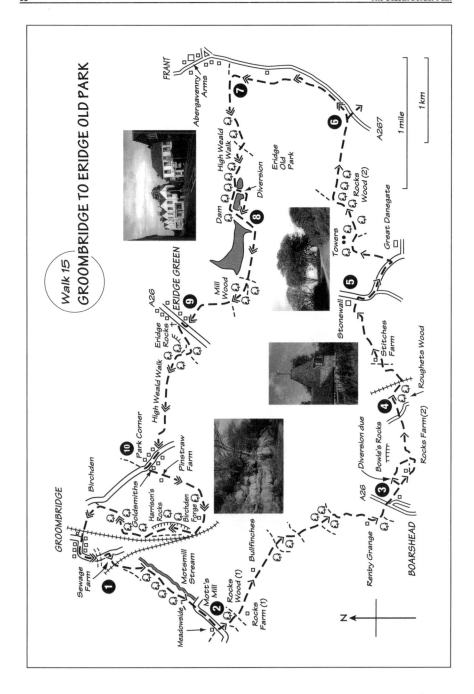

Walk 15
GROOMBRIDGE TO ERIDGE OLD PARK

follow the path beside the stream. Continue with the deer fence on your right. At the corner of the wood bear left through a gap in an old wire fence. Continue uphill, with the old fence on your right, to the A267.

6. Return: There is no right of way along the edge of the deer park, but access is allowed and a signboard shows the route. It is not waymarked, but there should be no difficulty if you turn left and follow a series of paths and tracks between the road and the deer park. The last section of the path runs close to the deer fence and joins the High Weald Walk at a gate. At this point you can continue the return trip or visit Frant.

Frant: Turn right uphill to the A267. Turn left and walk into Frant, where there is a village stores and **The Abergavenny Arms.**

7. Go through the gate into the park. From this point the return follows the High Weald Walk, which is well waymarked. Walk through the Park and then along the edge of a wood, where free range pigs may be seen. Where the open ground on the left ends, bear right into the wood. Cross a concrete bridge, and continue along a distinct path over a track. Continue beside the deer fence and along the edge of the wood, then turn left to cross the dam (in 1998 the dam was breached and the path had been diverted to turn left earlier – see map).

8. Go through a kissing gate and continue along the edge of a wood. Join a track and follow it round to the right and across a large field. At a T-junction of tracks turn right into

Mill Wood and follow the path through the wood and across a track. Bear right over a footbridge and continue uphill along the side of two fields. Take a gate on the right to join a track and turn left to the A26 at Eridge Green.

9. Turn right and then left just before Holy Trinity Church. Follow a private road to Eridge Rocks and take a path on the right below an outcrop, going uphill through woodland (if wet, stay on the road). Rejoin the road for a short distance and, where it swings right, turn left and cross two large fields. Turn right and then left through a strip of woodland and over a stream. Ignore a stile on the right and continue over a footbridge and the side of a field to a lane. Turn right to Park Corner, where the walk can be shortened by continuing along the road.

10. Just past Goldsmiths turn left along the private road to Pinstraw Farm and continue past the farm along a track. Follow a giant loop round past Birchden Forge to Harrison's Rocks, a popular climbing area. Instead of continuing along the Walk, take a path on the right below the Rocks, which at weekends are crowded with climbers but at other times have a quiet beauty. Rejoin the Walk and turn right to join the narrow road by the car park (in wet weather, avoid the path which cuts the corner). Continue to a metal gate just before a road and turn left along a path towards Groombridge. Cross the railway by a footbridge, turn left and follow the road back to the start.

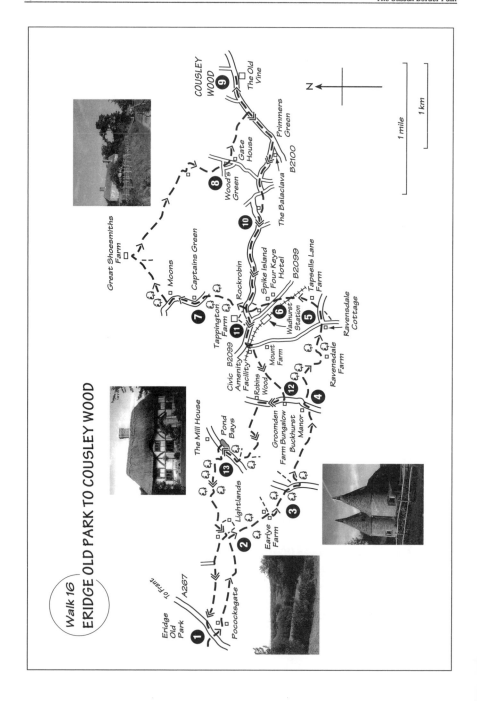

Walk 16
ERIDGE OLD PARK TO COUSLEY WOOD

16. Eridge Old Park to Cousley Wood

Distance: SBP: 10.5 km, 6.5 miles. **Return:** 8.0 km, 5.0 miles.

Maps: Explorer 136, Landranger 188.

En route: *Rockrobin:* hotel and inn.

Parking: lay-by on A267 south of start.

Things to see: Mount Farm and Linney Tea Room: 82 acres open to public, 7 Mar-Nov, school term Fri, Sat, Sun; school holidays – every day except Tues, 1000-1700, tel: 01892 783152.

This walk offers the same sort of rolling countryside as the previous one. In Spring bluebells, primroses, daffodils and snowdrops abound. The switch-back nature of the walk provides constantly changing views, but makes the going rather slower than might be expected.

1. SBP: Cross the A267 (583365) and take a track with a sign *Pococksgate.* Go between the farm buildings, along the top edges of two fields and through an orchard. Turn right and follow the edge of a field round to the left. Continue along the top of the next field, and cross another towards a house. Just before a stile by a private road, turn right along the edge of a field. This is not a right of way but a notice states that access is allowed.

2. Continue downhill through two fields to a wood. Cross a footbridge, climb steps, and cross a field towards Earlye Farm. Go through the buildings, to the left of a high-roofed barn, and continue along a track. Just past two oasts turn right and left into a field (this short zigzag is not apparent on OS maps). Follow the left edge of the field into a wood and continue downhill to a lane.

3. Turn right and follow the lane round to the right. Just before it

swings right again cross a stile on the left. Go downhill into a wood, and immediately turn left over a footbridge. Follow a path uphill through the wood to the corner of a field. Turn right and follow the edge of the field uphill. At the top move right into the adjoining field and continue along its left-hand edge. Bear slightly right past small sandstone outcrops to a gate. Continue along the edge of a field, and in the next bear left to its opposite corner and a lane.

4. Turn left, and opposite Buckhurst Manor cross a stile on the right. Follow the edge of a field downhill and at the bottom turn right into a wood. Go downhill, a little to the left, to a footbridge and bear left across the corner of a field. Continue across the corner of the next field into a strip of woodland and turn right by a stream. Turn left and cross the stream where sandstone slabs have been exposed by the water; there is no bridge. Go uphill along the edge of a field to a drive by Ravensdale Farm. Turn left and follow the drive uphill to a road by Ravensdale Cottage.

5. Cross the road and continue along a lane. Where it swings right, take a track on the left to Tapsells Lane Farm. Take a path to the left of the farm buildings and continue through woodland into a field. Cross a railway and go uphill to a road and the Four Keys hotel. Wadhurst station and the Rock Robin Inn- are a little further along the road to the north.

6. Turn left and just past the hotel take a track on the right to Spike Island, a house. Turn left in front of the house and cross the lawn to a path running parallel to the road. Continue along a metalled drive past Rock Robin Cott(age)s to a lane and turn right. Just past the private drive to Tappington Farm take a path on the left and follow it into a wood. Continue between fields and through another wood to a lane at Captains Green (a house) and turn left.

7. Follow the lane past Moons to the drive on the right to Great Shoesmiths Farm, and follow it almost to the farm buildings. Just before a garage turn right and go downhill past a pond. Cross a stream and bear left to cross a field to a gap in the hedge. In the next field bear a little to the right aiming to the right of a clump of trees. Continue along the edges of three more fields and then along a grassy track. Follow this round to the right to join a private road by a house. Turn left and go up-

hill past large houses to a junction of public roads at Wood's Green.

8. Turn left and shortly right at the next junction. Just past a converted barn turn left along a track. (it is worth making a short detour to see Gate House, the next building along). Follow a grassy track uphill and at the top bear right across a field. Continue along the edge of the next field and bear right across the next one. Continue to the B2100, and turn left to Cousley Wood (pronounced *cow*) and **The Old Vine**, a XVI century inn. Mind your head.

9. Return: Walk back along the B2100 towards Primmers Green. Turn right along Balaclava Lane, by a pub of the same name. Continue over a crossroads (signpost *Wadhurst Stn*) and at a T-junction continue along a path across a field. Continue along the edge of the next field and bear right to a lane.

10. Turn left downhill. Keep right at a junction (signpost *Wadhurst Station*), crossing the outward route at Rockrobin to join the B2029, just past the beautiful grounds of Tappington Farm.

11. Turn right and then left along Faircrouch Lane, over a railway bridge. Just past the Wadhurst Civic Amenity Facility turn right along a track and immediately right along a path (if you continue along the road you will come to the Mount Farm Tea Rooms in under 200 metres). Walk beside a fence with an excellent view over the Facility, and then bear slightly left across a field. Continue along the left side of the next field, go through a gate on the left into the adjoining field, and cross to its opposite corner. Cross a tiny stream (no bridge), turn right into a field and climb diagonally to its left-hand side. Continue along the edge of the next field to a lane by Groomden Farm Bungalow.

12. Turn right past Hillyfields Farm. At Robins Wood turn left, and follow the right edges of two fields. Cross the next small field to its opposite corner. Turn left over a footbridge and cross the corner of a field to a cattle trough. Bear right along the edge of the next field, cross a tiny stream and continue along the bottom of a field past a tennis court. Cross a footbridge into woodland and turn right to a track. Turn left, follow the track to a lane and turn right.

13. Just as a thatched house (The Mill House – well worth a detour) comes into view ahead, turn left along a path into woodland (possibly shown as open ground on the map). Follow the path round to the right and then to the left. At a fork go downhill to the right by a pond. Cross a footbridge and turn left into a field. Continue uphill along the edge of a field and follow it round to the left. Continue along the edge of the next field, and bear left uphill along the right edge of the next. At the top of the hill turn right along a private road and follow it round to the right, very close to the outward route. Follow the road uphill and at the top turn left along a path. Continue along a track to the A267, where a left turn will bring you back to the start.

The Mill House

17. Cousley Wood to Union Street (Bewl Water)

Distance: SBP: 10 km, 6 miles. **Return:** 12.5 km, 8 miles.
Flimwell: 1 km, 0.5 miles.

Maps: Explorer 136, Landranger 188.

En route: _Bewl Water Reservoir:_ see below. _Three Leg Cross:_ (return) pub. Teas at private house (see text and map).

Things to see: _Bewl Water Reservoir:_ Visitor Centre, tea room, toilets, Easter-Oct, winter weekends; cruises and ferry service on vintage boat, Apr-Sep, weekends Oct; woodland playground, picnic areas, ranger service, tel: 01892 890661. _Flimwell:_ Church of St Augustine.

This is essentially a walk round Bewl Water Reservoir. The going is mainly flat, apart from some road work on the return. The path round the reservoir is surfaced in parts, but elsewhere can be muddy. Scattered round the shore are small wooden huts, which provide rest and shelter, and toilets. It is the only walk for which a rescue service is available.

Because of the size of the reservoir, the walk is a long one. It can be broken into two by the following stratagem:

From **Cousley Wood**, walk to the visitor centre, take the ferry to the southern shore at Ferry Point and walk back round the western end of the reservoir.

From **Union Street**, proceed as above and walk back round the eastern end.

Check that you can land at Ferry Point. Note that you cannot board here.

1. SBP: Just past The Old Vine (651333) there is a private road with a sign _Little Butts Farm._ Follow this until it turns left, and keep straight on along a grassy track, with views over Bewl Water. At the top of a rise bear left and continue across a field. Follow a path downhill, go through a gap into a field and bear right. Go straight down towards the reservoir, along the edge of a field and a patch of uncultivated ground. At the bottom turn left.

2. Little description of the route is needed; just follow the path along the northern shore of the reservoir. Bewl Water is the largest area of inland water in south-east England, covering 770 acres. It was created between 1970 and 1975 by damming the River Bewl and now supplies large parts of Kent. The reservoir caters for many water sports, but no swimming is allowed.

3. At Hook House a metalled track leads uphill away from the reservoir.

The SBP between Bewl Water and Union Street

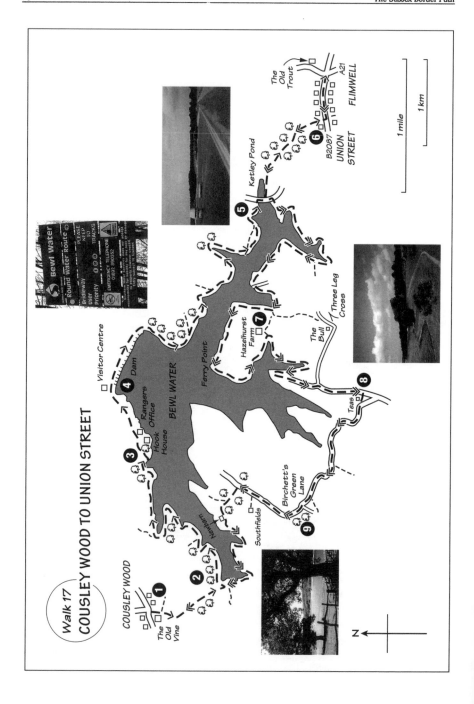

Walk 17
COUSLEY WOOD TO UNION STREET

Where this bends to the left, take steps going down the right. The SBP at this point is way-marked, and keeps closer to the reservoir than the route which may be shown on the map. Follow the path to a car park. The easiest course for the next few hundred yards is to follow the signs for the Round Bewl Water Walk to the Visitor Centre. Just past here, take steps down to the dam.

4. Follow the path along the dam and then along the shore. At the eastern end of the reservoir turn right along a road and continue over another, smaller dam.

5. A little past the dam, cross a stile on the left and follow a path east along the bottom of fields, with the tip of the reservoir on the left. Hedges and fences prevent you going astray. Cross a footbridge and stile and bear right towards a wood. Bear left over a footbridge and follow a distinct path through the wood. Where another path crosses, keep straight on uphill. Continue along a track with houses appearing on the right, to the B2087 at Union Street.

Flimwell: Turn left and walk along the B2087, where there is a village stores. For **The Old Trout**, turn left along the A21.

6. Return: Walk back to the small dam. The route of the Round Bewl Water Walk has been adopted. This is well signposted where signposts are needed, which is not very often. Turn left and follow the path along the southern shore of the reservoir. Again, few directions are needed.

7. As Hazelhurst Farm is approached, the Bewl Water Walk turns left (a footpath goes straight on round Ferry Point – the detour is worth doing). Follow the path past the farm to rejoin the shore. (a detour can be made from here to The Bull at Three Leg Cross). At a sign *Nature Reserve Please Keep Out* turn sharp back left along the path and then along a metalled road. Keep right at a fork and continue to a row of houses, the last of which sells refreshments and offers B and B.

8. The official walk can be short cut by taking a footpath just past this house on the right, going beside its garden and through two fields to rejoin the road. Turn right, and follow Birchett's Green Lane for one and a half kilometres to a fork.

9. At the fork, turn right at a signpost *Ward's Lane* and continue past Southfields. Just past a wood turn left down a private road to Newbarn (Newborn?). Go downhill, enjoying views over the reservoir, to a track leading to the shore. Turn left and walk along the shore. The path back to Cousley Wood is easily missed – take care, it would be a pity to go round twice by mistake. At the western end of the reservoir, look out for a sign *Footpath to Wadhurst*. A little past this there is a triangle of grass and, some way from the shore path, a sign. Turn left and follow the SBP back to Cousley Wood.

18. Union Street to Bodiam

Distance: SBP: 12.5 km, 8 miles. **Return:** same.

Maps: Explorer 136, Landranger 188.

En route: *The Moor:* pub and shops.

Things to see: *The Moor:* Church of St. Laurence. *Bodiam:* Bodiam Castle: (NT), XIV century, 14 Feb-1 Nov daily, 3 Nov-3 Jan daily exc. Mon, 1000-1600 or dusk, tel: 01580 830436.

This walk is one of the best, through beautiful rolling countryside with constantly changing views, which culminate at Bodiam Castle. No return route can be devised without excessive road walking, but it is no hardship to follow the SBP back. This is a long walk, which can be split at The Moor.

---

1. SBP: Take a track (709312) opposite a house called Toad Hall and follow it past Quedley. Just past a flagstaff take a grassy path on the left and follow it round to the right. Continue along the edge of a golf course (which may not be shown as such on the map). If you thought golf was played for exercise you may change your mind. Follow a metalled track for a short distance to a junction. Bear right, to the left of a large silver birch, to a signpost at the edge of a wood. One arm points in the wrong direction, NW, although the path heads SW into the wood (1998). Follow the path through the wood, negotiating fallen trees, to a field. Take the left-hand of two paths and go downhill to the corner. Cross a footbridge in a strip of woodland and go uphill along the edge of a field (where the map may show a wood) and across another strip of woodland. Continue along the edge of a field bearing right and then left. At the top cross three stiles in rapid succession, with Roughfield on the right, and follow a path through woodland. Turn left along a track and follow it up a hill. Just before the top turn right into a field and very shortly cross a stile on the left and follow a path to the A21.

2. Cross, turn right and walk a short distance to a gate opposite the Woodland Enterprise Centre. Navigation by Roughfield Farm and Brookgate Farm needs care, and the good-natured folk who live there must spend much of their time giving directions to errant walkers. Cross a field to the end of an overgrown hedge. Bear right along a track leading away from the hedge to a junction of tracks by a cattle-trough. Cross a track and continue along the top of a long narrow field. Continue through the next field along a grassy track, with a wood on the left. A little way into the next field cross a stile on

Bodiam Castle

the left and cross a field to a gap in the hedge (make a mental note of this for the return). Turn right along the edge of a field to Brookgate Farm.

3. There is a special enlarged section of the map showing the route through the farm – the easy way, not the right-of-way. Go past the first group of buildings and where the track turns right continue past another building. Turn right, then left up the drive towards the farmhouse. Just before the house turn right and then left onto a track (the track further south by converted oasts is impassable). Continue for a short distance and, by a large wooden bridge on the right, take a footbridge (which may be hidden by foliage) almost straight ahead. Go through a

small wood into a field, cross diagonally and continue along the right edges of two fields into a patch of woodland. Just before a large house on the left turn right over a footbridge and go along the edge of a field. Continue along the right edge of the next field. Turn left along a grassy track and almost immediately right through a gap in the hedge. Cross the corner of a field, follow the right edge of the next for a short distance and then go straight across to a gate and a lane by Hurstwood Cottage.

4. Turn left and almost immediately right into an orchard (the map may show another orchard on the right which is now a field). Continue with a tall hedge on the right and at its end

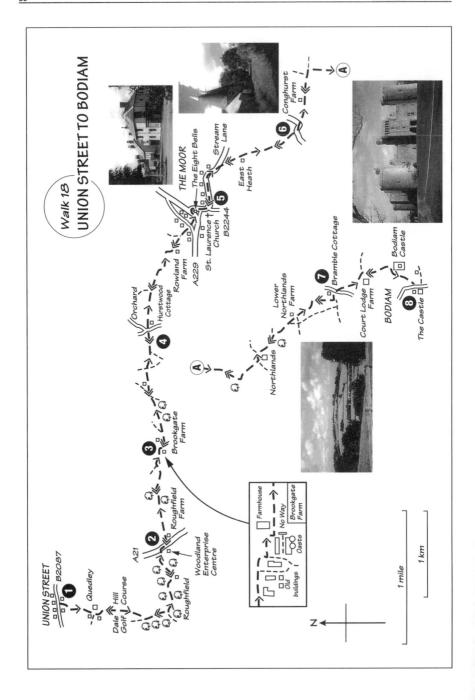

Walk 18
UNION STREET TO BODIAM

move a little to the right and continue to the end of the orchard. Continue through woodland under a fallen tree. Turn right into a field and follow its right edge. In the next field turn left, and in the next right towards Rowland Farm. Before reaching the buildings cross a stile on the left and follow a path which by-passes the farm buildings. Just before the corner of the field move right to join the farm track and continue along it to a lane by a weather-boarded cottage. Turn right along the lane to a road. Turn right again and immediately left along a road which brings you to the A229 in The Moor. The Eight Bells is just to the left, and there is a shop on the other side of the green. Cross the A229 and go along a minor road past the church of St. Laurence.

5. Cross the B2244 and go down Stream Lane. Follow the lane round to the right and take a gravel drive on the right with a sign *East Heath*. At East Heath continue along a path between fields and past a wood on the left. Cross a bridge and continue uphill to a lane.

6. Turn left and follow the lane for a short distance until it turns left. Take a private road on the right to Conghurst Farm. Pass a house incorporating five oasts and continue through the farm buildings to follow a track downhill. About a hundred metres before the bottom, take a track on the right, with a prominent white house ahead. Follow the edge cf a field and go to the left of a fence at the bottom of a hill. At the corner move right up a bank to cross a

bridge and continue uphill along the edge of a field. Turn left beside a wooden fence, bear round to the right and continue towards Northlands. Turn left in front of the farm buildings and just past the last building, which is a stable block, turn right along the edge of a field. Continue past a wood, cross a bridge and go uphill. At the top, there is a house which may not appear on the map. At Lower Northlands Farm continue through a small wooden gate to a private road and follow this to a road at Bramble Cottage.

7. Turn right and almost immediately take a path on the left going diagonally uphill across a field. Turn left along the bottom of the next field, then turn right uphill. Cross the drive of Court Lodge Farm and a small area of grass, and go downhill along the edge of a field. If you look back at the house you will see that it incorporates three oasts, each with a weathervane with a different animal: a pig, a horse and a cow. The great bulk of Bodiam Castle comes into view. Halfway down the field follow a separate path at its edge. At the bottom of the field, turn right into the grounds of Bodiam Castle – one of the last great mediaeval castles to be built and a justifiably popular NT property. There is a museum in the building to the right. Go to the right of the moat towards a car park and into **Bodiam**. The NT provide a restaurant, a shop and toilets. There is another restaurant and a pub, The Castle, which offers speciality sausages, and duck and goose eggs when available.

Oasts, Court Lodge

8. Return: walks can seem quite different when reversed, so a brief description of the return route is given.

From Bodiam Castle, go uphill to Court Lodge Farm, and bear left downhill to Bramble Cottage.

7. Cross the lane and follow the private road to Lower Northlands Farm. Continue uphill to Northlands and turn left past the buildings, then right downhill by a wooden fence. Turn right at a wood, go downhill then up and continue to a track. Turn left to Conghurst Farm and a lane.

6. Continue along the lane to a bend to the left, and continue along a path to East Heath and then Stream Lane. Turn left to The Moor.

5. Go past the church, cross the A229 and another road, and follow the track to Rowland Farm. Take a path to the right of the farm, and go right, left, right and left along the edges of fields to an orchard. Go through the orchard and cross a lane at Hurstwood Cottage.

4. Follow a path through fields to a patch of woodland by a large house. Bear left and continue to Brookgate Farm.

3. A little past the farm, bear left through a gap and cross a field. Continue to the A21 and turn right.

2. Take a path beside a cottage. Turn right and left and follow a track to Roughfield. Before the house, take a path on the right. Go downhill to a footbridge, then bear right uphill into a wood. Go through the wood to the golf course, and cross it to Quedley. Follow a track back to Union Street.

19. Bodiam to Beckley

Distance: SBP: 10 km, 6 miles. **Return:** 9.5 km, 6 miles.

Maps: Explorer 136 and 125, Landranger 199.

Parking: there is free parking south of Bodiam Bridge.

En route: *Ewhurst Green:* inn/restaurant. *Northiam:* hotel, pub, shops.

Things to see: *Ewhurst Green:* Church of St. James the Great. *Northiam:* Church of St Mary; *Great Dixter:* XV century timber-framed house with Great Hall, restored and enlarged, ever-changing gardens, 1 Apr-25 Oct, 1400-1700 except Mon, tel: 01797 252878; *Brickwall:* timber-framed Jacobean house and gardens, by appointment, tel: 01797 223329.

This walk is similar to the previous one. It goes through varied countryside with some of the best views on the SBP. The return includes a long tramp along a lane, but it is quiet and gives excellent views.

1. SBP: Cross the bridge over the Rother (783253), turn left and follow a path along the embankment. Just before a ditch turn right and follow the edges of a field to double metal gates. Cross a disused railway, go through a small wooden gate, cross a stile and turn right behind a barn to a footbridge. Follow the edge of a field to another footbridge, turn left and shortly cross a stile. Cross a field to its top left-hand corner. Follow the left edge of the next field to a stile. Go through a strip of woodland and turn right along the edge of a field. At the top of the field there are views of the valley of the Rother and Bodiam Castle.

2. Turn left along a road and walk through Ewhurst Green, a pleasant village with some attractive old houses. Just past the White Dog turn

right downhill, along the edge of a field. Do not continue to the bottom; turn left over a footbridge into the adjoining field and continue along its lower edge. Pass an orchard and at its corner turn right along a path beside a lane.

3. Turn right along the lane and shortly, just before a bridge, take a path on the left. Continue along the edge of a field, beside a stream, and in the corner cross a footbridge on the right. Turn left and cross the corner of a field to a footbridge. Do not cross; turn right along the edge of the field with the stream on your left (the path over the bridge leads to Great Dixter). Go through a strip of woodland and cross a field. Cross a footbridge, and follow the edge of a field with the stream and trees on your left. Look out for a footbridge on the

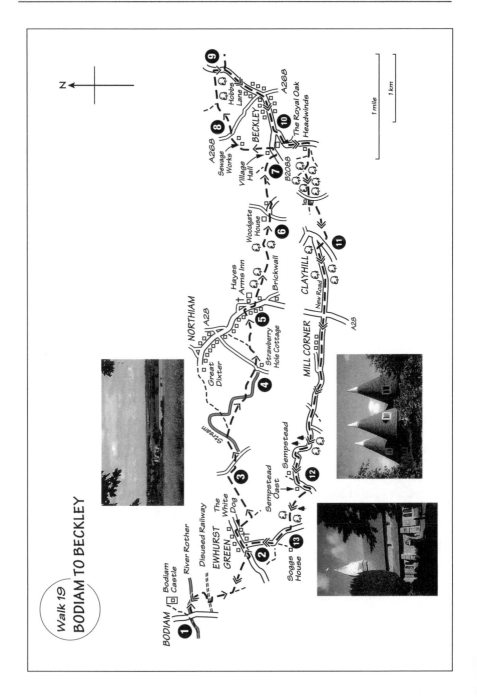

Walk 19
BODIAM TO BECKLEY

N

1 mile
1 km

BODIAM
Bodiam Castle
River Rother
Disused Railway
EWHURST GREEN
The White Dog
Soggs House
Sempstead Oast
Sempstead
Stream
Great Dixter
NORTHIAM
A28
Strawberry Hole Cottage
Hayes Arms Inn
Brickwall
Woodgate House
MILL CORNER
New Road
CLAYHILL
A28
Sewage Works
A268
Hobbs Lane
Village Hall
BECKLEY
B2088
The Royal Oak
Headwinds
A268

Church of St James the Great, Ewhurst Green

of the field, cross a strip of woodland and continue between fields towards a church spire. Continue along a drive to the A28 at Northiam and turn right.

5. Just past the Hayes Arms Inn, turn left along a drive by a triangle of grass and turn right into a field. Turn left and follow the edge of the field to its corner. Cross the next field and then follow its edge. Go between twin power lines, bear slightly left across a field and follow a path through a wood. Bear right over a footbridge, turn left along the edge of a field for a short distance and then bear right along a path across its corner. Continue along the right edge of the next field and the left edge of the next. Cross a stile to a lane by Woodgate House. Turn left and almost immediately right along Rectory Lane.

left and cross it. Turn right and continue, with the stream now on the right, to a lane.

4. Cross and take a path which runs beside the drive to Strawberry Hole Cottage (*not* Strawberry Hole). Cross the corner of a field, and in the next bear left uphill along an obvious path. Just before the top, turn right at a waymark post (for Northiam, keep straight on). Continue to the corner

6. Just past the grounds of a large white house turn left into a drive. Cross a stile behind a stable block (which may not appear on the map), cross a field and continue across another to a stile just before its far corner. Bear round to the left past a patch of woodland and cross the next field diagonally. Continue, beside a bungalow on the left, to the B2088 at Beckley and turn left.

7. Just past the Village Hall, turn left into an old orchard and follow its edge beside a stream. Cross the stream by a farm bridge, and continue with the stream on the right. Re-cross by a footbridge and continue below sewage works. Continue uphill, bear right past a barn and continue across fields to the A268.

8. Turn right and shortly left opposite a cottage. Cross a field to a stile, cross the corner of the next field and go uphill across the next. Go through a strip of woodland, cross a field, bear right beside a wood and continue to a lane (Hobbs Lane). Turn right.

9. Return: continue along the lane, cross the A268, and follow the B2088 through Beckley, where there is a village stores (good pasties) and **The Royal Oak.**

10. Take Kings Bank Lane to the left of the pub. Beside the drive to Headwinds take a path on the right, where an odd detour is necessary to keep to the right-of-way. Just past a tall hedge, cross a stile on the right and continue across the corner of a field to another stile. Continue across the corner of the next field and follow a path into a wood. Cross a footbridge and follow the path through the wood. Continue along the edge of a field to a lane. Turn left and almost immediately take a path on the right. At its end turn left over a stile and double back to a cattle trough. In the next field turn right along the edge to

a stile almost concealed in its corner, and in the next bear a little away from the edge to a gap in the hedge. Bear right across the next field to a foot bridge, cross a track and continue along the edge of a field. Bear right by houses to a lane at Clay Hill.

11. Turn left and immediately take a short path on the right to a lane (New Road). Turn left and follow the lane for four kilometres. Cross the A28 and continue past Mill Corner, where a lane joins from the right. Continue past another lane from Northiam on the right. At the next junction keep right, signpost *Ewhurst*, along Sempstead Lane. The lane winds downhill and up. Switch your brain on again as you pass Sempstead and a path on the right.

12. Continue uphill past Sempstead Oast, where the right-of-way has been diverted to the south (1998). Where the lane swings right, turn right into a field and go downhill along its edge. At the bottom bear right to a stile and continue along the edge of Stumblott's Wood. Turn left by the corner of a field, cross a grassy track and continue downhill, keeping right. Continue along a path between fields.

13. Turn right along a lane, and continue to Ewhurst Green. Turn left, and just past the last house turn right and follow the SBP back to Bodiam.

Note: Local residents state (1998) that the right of way which begins at the drive to Soggs House is (a) impassable and (b) due to be diverted.

20. Beckley to Rye

Distance: SBP: 13 km, 8 miles. **Return:** 10 km, 6 miles.

Maps: Explorer 125, Landranger 189.

Parking: There is very limited parking on the verges of Hobbs Lane south of the start. The best plan is to start from Beckley.

Things to see: *Rye*: Heritage Centre (and Tourist Information Centre): daily, tel: 01797 226696; Rye Castle Museum: Easter-31 Oct, 1030-1730, winter weekends 1030-1600, tel: 01797 226728; Church of St Mary and Ypres Tower: daily 1000-dusk, tel: 01797 222340; Rye Treasury of Mechanical Music: Mar to Oct daily 1000-1700, Nov-Feb 1100-1600 except Tue, tel: 01797 223345; Rye Art Galleries: daily, tel: 01797 222433.

A river flowing through flat countryside does not usually make for exciting walking, and the Rother is no exception. After the start the route is quite level, allowing fast progress. It runs through what was once the bed of the sea, and the old shore-line is clearly visible on both sides. There are some good views on the return.

---

1. SBP: To start from Beckley, cross the A268, walk up Hobbs Lane and take a path on the right (865247) just past Hobbs Farm. To continue from the previous walk, follow the lane until it swings right and take a path on the left just past a cottage (865247). Follow the upper edge of a field and in the next field turn right and then left along its edges. Continue through a wood to a field and bear a little to the right. In the next field, which contains a number of oak trees, bear left to its far corner. Continue along the edge of the next field and bear right across the next to its corner, by a prominent willow. Cross a footbridge and turn right over a farm bridge. Go through a gate into the next field and immediately turn left. When the fence swings left keep

straight on, and cross a small field to a track beside a barn (which, with the house on the right, may not appear on the map). Bear left across a field, aiming to the left of a clump of trees, and go through a small wood to a lane at Blackwall Cottage. Turn left and continue to Blackwall Bridge and the River Rother.

2. Cross the bridge and turn right along the embankment. Little guidance is necessary, for the SBP follows the river bank all the way to Rye. The deviation from the river which may appear on the map is not followed in practice.

3. At the B2082 take the path beside the river, not the track. At the next bridge, detour round a house, and cross the Military Road and the

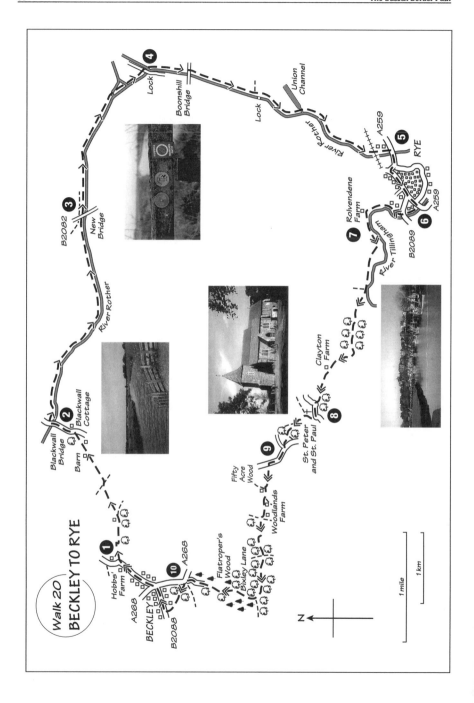

Walk 20
BECKLEY TO RYE

The River Rother near its junction with the Royal Military Canal

Royal Military Canal, which runs from Hythe to Cliff End near Hastings. The Canal was built during the Napoleonic Wars to serve both as a means of transport and a barrier in the event of a French invasion. When the risk of invasion had gone, the Canal was opened for public use. It is now important as a means of controlling the water level in the marshes.

4. The next section of the SBP is shared by the Royal Military Canal Path and the Saxon Shore Way. At the next lock Rye appears on the horizon, and the river becomes tidal. Continue across the Union Channel. Near Rye, drop to the bank to duck under a rail bridge.

5. At the road bridge, turn right along the A259 into **Rye**. The town was once an important seaport on a promontory, which made it easy to defend. Because of silting and a shifting coastline it is now inland, although still used by fishing craft. It is a fascinating place with mediaeval buildings, city walls and narrow cobbled streets. There are many places of interest, usually thronged with tourists. Hotels, pubs and restaurants abound. The original guide does not mention an 'official' end to the SBP; the map ends at the railway station. A visit to the Ypres Tower, which dominates the sky-line for the final section, is suggested. There are plenty of signs to direct you there, and you can gaze nostalgically back over the final section of the walk.

6. **Return:** Make your way to the west side of Rye, where the A259 crosses the River Tillingham. Just before the

bridge, take a path on the right towards a windmill and follow it beside the river, crossing a railway and the B2089.

7. Below Rolvendene farm turn left, and continue through a field, which is also a camp site, by the river. Take the left-hand of two gates and continue beside a drainage channel. Follow this round to the right to a gate. Bear left across a field to a gate beside the river. Bear right away from the river to a footbridge, climb a hill and follow a track through an orchard. Continue along the track for one-and-a-half kilometres, past Clayton Farm to a lane.

8. Turn left and continue to the Church of St Peter and St Paul. Turn right into the churchyard, walk round the church, and take a path going NW beside a power line. Where this swings right, bear slightly left. Go through a gate in a dip and continue along an imposing avenue of lime trees to a junction of lanes.

9. Continue along the lane. Just before Fifty Acre Wood, take a track on the left to Woodlands Farm. *Note: OS maps show a more direct route from this point NW to Beckley, but there are difficulties in the woodland north of the A268.* There is a sign *Private No Car Access*, but not the name of the farm. Continue past the farmhouse and through the farm buildings. Just past here the track swings right. Take the middle of three tracks into a wood and almost immediately take a faint path on the left to the corner of the wood. Continue across a hop-field, the northern section of which has been planted with young

(in 1998) trees, so that the right-of-way cannot be followed exactly. Cross a stile near the far right corner, bear right to a wide path, turn left and follow it through woodland. Cross another path and continue through a kissing gate, where the path becomes narrower. This wood is managed as a reserve by the Sussex Wildlife Trust. Cross a stream and immediately keep left at a fork. Continue under power lines to a track (Bixley Lane), turn right and continue to a lane and the A268.

10. Just before the main road take a path on the left into a wood and immediately fork right. Follow an obvious path, and just past a wooden seat take a stile on the right into a field. This field may appear as an orchard on older maps, and to confuse matters further the southern tip has been planted with young (in 1998) trees. Turn right and follow a path along the edge of a field. Cross a stile on the right and follow a path to the B2088 at Beckley.

The Mid-Sussex Link

The Sussex Border Path south of Horsted Keynes (Walk 23)

21. East Grinstead to Sharpthorne

Distance: SBP: 9 km, 5.5 miles. **Return:** 9.5 km, 6 miles.

Maps: Explorer 135 (18), Landranger 187.

Parking: near roundabout on outskirts of East Grinstead.

Things to see: *Bluebell Railway:* stations at Sheffield Park, Horsted Keynes and Kingscote (no road access); vintage bus service: Kingscote to East Grinstead; open daily May-Sep and school holidays, every weekend at other times; address: The Bluebell Railway, Sheffield Park Station, East Sussex, TN22 3QL, tel: 01825 722370 (24-hour time-table), 01825 723777 (enquiries). *Standen:* XIX century house, centre of Arts and Crafts movement, garden and woodland walks, restaurant, open 25 Mar-1 Nov, Wed-Sun, 1230-1600, tel: 01342 323029.

This walk provides varied scenery with fine views throughout. It includes one of the largest stretches of water on the SBP, Weir Wood Reservoir. Several sandstone outcrops are passed. Nearby is the Bluebell Railway, one of the oldest and best known preserved lines, whose steam engines provide cheerful background noises on this and the following walks.

This walk can be combined with the next, using the railway services to return to East Grinstead from Horsted Keynes. It is a pity that the short section of the return through Ashdown Forest is not representative of the excellent walking over most of the Forest.

1. SBP: From the traffic lights (393381) in East Grinstead (Walk 12), walk up London Road to High Street and turn left. Continue past magnificent old buildings to a roundabout, and turn right down a tarmac path signposted as a cycle way to Forest Row. Continue past an unusual modern signpost into the Forest Way Country Park and follow an old railway embankment for one-and-a-half kilometres. Go under a bridge, turn right up steps to a private road, and turn left.

2. Weir Wood Reservoir can be seen ahead. Follow the road downhill and just past Horseshoe Cottage turn right along a path between yews. Continue over a footbridge, where another path crosses, and along the edges of two fields. Cross the next field aiming for a sign to the right of Busses Farm. Turn left and follow a concrete track round to the right with the farm buildings on the left. Turn left at the end of the buildings to a track leading downhill towards the reservoir. At the corner of a field,

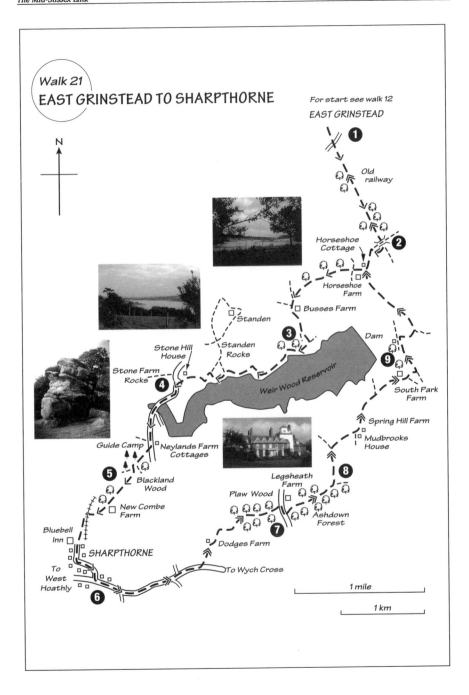

Walk 21
EAST GRINSTEAD TO SHARPTHORNE

For start see walk 12
EAST GRINSTEAD

N

1

Old railway

Horseshoe Cottage

2

Horseshoe Farm

Busses Farm

Standen

3

Dam

9

South Park Farm

Stone Hill House

Standen Rocks

Stone Farm Rocks

4

Weir Wood Reservoir

Spring Hill Farm

Mudbrooks House

Guide Camp

Neylands Farm Cottages

5

Blackland Wood

New Combe Farm

Legsheath Farm

Plaw Wood

8

Ashdown Forest

7

Bluebell Inn

SHARPTHORNE

Dodges Farm

To West Hoathly

To Wych Cross

6

1 mile

1 km

keep left beside the hedge. The map may show the SBP going across the field to the right.

3. Where the path meets another turn right and continue through woodland and fields, with the reservoir on your left. The reservoir was created between 1950 and 1954 by damming the River Medway, and straddles the border between East and West Sussex. The eastern end is used for fishing and sailing; the western end is a nature reserve where many species of bird may be seen. There is no public access to the water itself, and the sense of being welcome, felt at Bewl Water, is noticeably lacking. Where power lines cross the path Standen Rocks appear on the right and may be visited by a short detour. Continue to a lane, turn right and continue to a road.

A short detour is worthwhile at this point. Turn right up the hill to Stonehill (Stone Hill?) House and take a track opposite. At a sign *Stone Farm Rocks*, take a footpath on the left and walk along to admire the rocks and enjoy an extensive view over the reservoir.

4. Turn left and follow the road downhill past the end of the reservoir. Pass Legsheath Lane and ascend the hill. Just past Neylands Farm Cottages, take a path on the right through a Guide Camp. The site buildings may not appear on older maps.

5. At the edge of the site, cross a track into Blackland Wood, and go downhill to the left, ignoring a smaller track on the right. Cross a footbridge and bear right to follow a path up-

Rocks, Stone Farm

hill. Leave the wood and cross a field to join a concrete track at the corner of a wood and follow it below New Coombe Farm. Go under the Bluebell Railway, and follow the track round to the left. Continue into Sharpthorne and **The Bluebell Inn**, the only pub on this walk. Follow the road round to the left and then to the right to join the main road by a shop. To continue the SBP turn right; for the return walk turn left.

6. Return: Follow the road east for over a kilometre (signpost *Wych Cross* and *Forest Row*), passing two lanes on the right and one on the left, and take a track on the left with a sign *Dodges Farm*. Just before buildings turn right along a track and very shortly cross a stile on the left. Cross the corners of two fields and turn right along a path downhill, bearing left and then right into Plaw Wood. Follow the path uphill through the wood and keep right at a fork, along a path which may be overgrown in summer. Turn left when the path meets another and continue to a lane by Legsheath Farm.

7. Turn right and, just past an Ashdown Forest sign and a wooden fence, turn left along a (possibly overgrown) path into the Forest, and follow it downhill. When open ground appears on the left look out for a low concrete Public Footpath sign and a stile on the left.

8. Cross the stile and follow a path downhill through rough ground to a footbridge. Cross a field steeply uphill and continue across another field. Cross the next field to the right of a pond. Bear right over the brow of

the hill, where Weir Wood Reservoir re-appears, to a stile on the right, where two rights of way diverge. Take the one on the right (no path is visible) across the field. Go downhill across the next field to Mudbrooks House. Turn left along a track through Spring Hill Farm and past South Park Farm.

9. Where the track swings right take a path on the left into a wood. Continue to a road beside a house and turn left. At a brick wall with gates, take a path on the right parallel to the road and continue to a stream. Do not cross; turn right and follow the bank to cross a footbridge on the left. Follow the path round to the left and climb to another footpath. Turn left and follow the footpath beside the stream and then though fields to Horseshoe Farm. Turn right to rejoin the SBP and retrace your steps to East Grinstead.

22. Sharpthorne to Horsted Keynes

Distance: SBP: 5.5 km, 3.5 miles. **Return:** 10 km, 6 miles.

Maps: Explorer 135 (18), Landranger 187.

Things to see: *Horsted Keynes:* Church of St. Giles. Broadhurst Manor: timber-framed mansion, by appointment, tel: 01342 810596. *West Hoathly:* guided tours of village, tel. 01342 810479; The Priest House: XV century timber-framed farmhouse, museum, cottage and herb gardens, Mar-Oct 1100-1730, Suns 1400-1730; The Manor House: XVII century stone-built, not open to the public; Church of St. Margaret: XIII century, terraced churchyard.

This walk goes through typical rolling Sussex countryside and is a delight throughout. The SBP section is short; the return longer. The going is good with the possible exception of mud in the final stretch of woodland.

---

1. SBP: From the end of the previous walk (373324), go west towards the centre of Sharpthorne and take a drive on the left between the Sharpthorne Club and a garage. Behind the club turn left and right along a path which goes downhill between tall hedges, and continue along the edge of a field. There are good views to the South Downs. Cross another field, and at the corner of Moon's Wood bear right over a stream. Cross the next three fields diagonally and go downhill along the edge of the next field to a metalled drive by Claverdale, a house which may not appear on older maps. Turn left and walk to a public road.

2. Turn right along the road. Just before Saxons (a house which offers B and B) take a path on the left across a field into a wood (it is worth continuing a few yards along the road to see Tanyard Manor). Cross a dam and

immediately turn left and then right to the top of the wood. Turn left and then right along the edges of a field, then go into a wood and over a footbridge. Ascend to a field and turn left and right along its edges to a lane.

3. Turn right and then left at a junction, signposted *Birch Grove*. Turn right at a sign *Broadhurst Manor*. In front of the manor, which is now an animal sanctuary, turn right along a drive with a stone wall on the left. Just before a timber-framed house turn left down a track. Continue past a series of ponds, which were first constructed to provide a reserve of water for the hammer pond, the lowest, which powered the forges and the great hammers of the Sussex iron industry. They are now the preserve of local anglers. The track climbs to join a road at the outskirts of **Horsted Keynes**. Continue past the Church of St Giles and climb a hill by the mag-

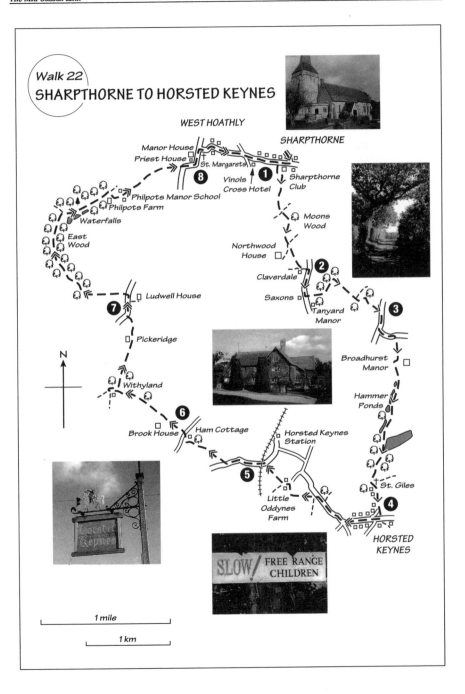

Walk 22

SHARPTHORNE TO HORSTED KEYNES

WEST HOATHLY

SHARPTHORNE

Manor House
Priest House
St. Margarets

8

Vinols
Cross Hotel

1

Sharpthorne
Club

Philpots Manor School
Philpots Farm
Waterfalls

East
Wood

Moons
Wood

Northwood
House

Claverdale

2

Saxons

Tanyard
Manor

3

Ludwell House

7

Broadhurst
Manor

Pickeridge

N

Hammer
Ponds

Withyland

6

Brook House

Ham Cottage

Horsted Keynes
Station

5

St. Giles

Little
Oddynes
Farm

4

HORSTED
KEYNES

1 mile

1 km

SLOW! FREE RANGE CHILDREN

nificent grounds of The Old Rectory. Where the road swings right keep straight on along a path. A left turn will bring you to two pubs, The Green Man and The Crown, and the village stores. For the SBP cross to the Post Office.

4. Return: From the Post Office, walk west along the road (signposted *Horsted Keynes Station*) and turn right down Waterbury Hill. Just over a bridge there is a concrete track on the left; from it take a footpath going up across a field on the right. At the far corner of the field bear right along a track to Little Oddynes Farm. At the farmhouse, turn left and immediately right, then left again between farm buildings and right past the last building. Cross the corner of a field and bear right across the next field to a railway bridge.

5. Turn left along a lane and follow it to a stile on the right. Follow a path which edges away from the road and bear slightly right across the next, large field (in which trees had been planted in 1998). Cross a track and go downhill between fields into woodland. Cross another track and continue uphill along a path and then a track. Then, turn right into the garden of Ham Cottage and bear left to a lane.

6. Turn right and almost immediately left up steps and continue along the edge of a field. Follow the edge of the next field above Brook House and just before its end turn left through a kissing gate to the corner of a cricket ground. Bear right behind the pavilion to another kissing gate behind a bush on the right. Cross a field diago-

nally into woodland and go downhill over a brick footbridge. Continue uphill to Withyland and, at the top of the field beside the house, double back down the other side (the route followed by rights of way is not my responsibility) and bear left into a wood. The next section is waymarked High Weald Landscape Trail and High Weald Circular Walks. Bear left again over a footbridge and continue along the edges of two fields and across another to Pickeridge (Farmhouse). Continue along a track to a lane and turn right.

7. Just past Ludwell House take a gate on the left and follow the edge of a field. Cross the next field to a wood, aiming to the left of trees which protrude into the field. Bear right and follow a broad path downhill through the wood. Cross a footbridge and continue uphill. Walk a few paces along a track which immediately swings right, and continue along the path. Bear right, downhill, and cross a private track, where the High Weald waymarking leads elsewhere. Continue uphill with only glimpses of the waterfalls. At the top keep right below houses. Pass farm buildings, turn left along a track, and follow it round to the left past Philpots Manor School. Follow the track until it joins a lane, and continue to West Hoathly, with its old buildings and the Cat Inn.

8. Turn right past the church and follow the road to the Vinols Cross Hotel. Bear right and follow the road downhill into Sharpthorne.

23. Horsted Keynes to Scaynes Hill

Distance: SBP: 9.5 km, 6.0 miles. **Return:** 7 km, 4.5 miles.

Maps: Explorer 135 (18), Landranger 198.

En route: *Freshfield:* pub.

Things to see: *Scaynes Hill:* Rock Lodge Vineyard: weekdays 1100-1700, tel: 01444 831567.

This walk passes through pleasant rolling countryside with good views both north and south. The Bluebell Railway is crossed on both the outward and return routes. A word of warning – if the walks were graded for mud this one would earn four stars.

---

1. SBP: Behind the Post Office (383282) take Chapel Lane, a track. Follow Wyatt's Lane round to the right and continue along a track by a sign *Private Road To Wyatts.* At a junction with another track keep right and continue downhill. Keep left where a footpath goes off to the right and continue through a wood, which can be very muddy. Continue between fields and bear left over Danehill Brook. Climb steeply and follow the track round to the left, then turn right uphill by the entrance to Hole House. Continue uphill along a metalled track and at the top of the hill, where the track swings right, continue along a path to Freshfield Lane.

2. Turn right past April Cottage and then left along a drive with a sign *Butchers Barn.* Just over a bridge, as buildings come into view, take a footpath on the left along the edge of a field, with the buildings on the right. Follow the path round to the right above a pond and turn left along the edge of the next field (this is not

quite as shown on the map, although there has not been a diversion) to Heaven Wood. Turn sharp right along the edge of the wood and continue past Northland Farm to a lane by Kingswood Cottage. Cross to a path into King's Wood, and immediately turn right. Walk through the wood and cross a field to the corner of another wood, where the path joins a track. Continue beside the wood and fork right under the Bluebell Railway.

3. Bear right along the edge of a wood and over a farm bridge. Bear left across a field to a footbridge halfway across and continue, aiming to the right of Freshfield Mill Farm. Cross two small fields by the buildings and turn left along a road.

4. Cross a bridge over the River Ouse and walk past The Sloop. Just past the first house on the left, turn left along a track with a sign *Field Cottage* and continue into Hammer Wood. A little way into the wood, by a short section of track, cross a stile

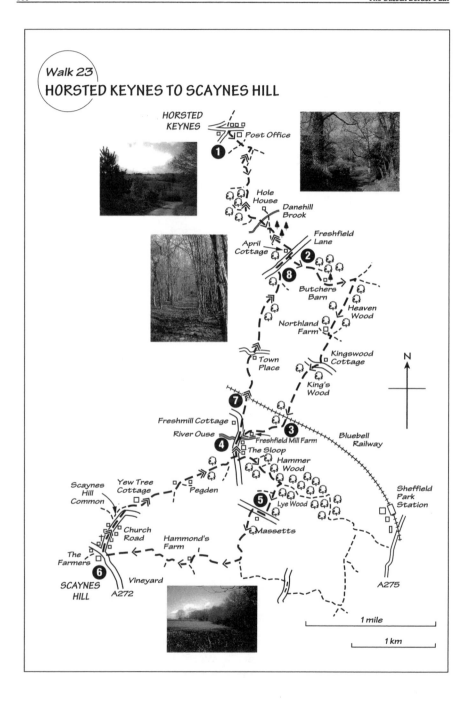

Walk 23
HORSTED KEYNES TO SCAYNES HILL

on the right and follow a path uphill and over a stile. Continue uphill to the corner of a field and turn right and then left along its edges. Turn right at a gap in the hedge into an open area ringed by trees and cross to a cattle trough. Bear left along the edge of a field into Lye Wood. Follow a path through the wood and then along the edge of a field to a lane.

5. Turn right and, a little past Massetts, cross a stile on the left and continue along the left edge of a field. Follow the edge of the next field round to the right, ignoring a stile at its corner. Turn left through a gate into another field and bear left across it, aiming for a point about halfway along its opposite side, where there is a signpost. Turn right along the edge of the field down to a stile but do not cross. Instead, turn right and cross the field bearing away from its bottom to a stile and a gate. Cross the corner of the next field to a signpost and follow its edge uphill. At the top cross a stile, turn right, and walk round three sides of a field, passing the buildings of Hammond's Farm on the right. Turn right to join a track at a turning circle. Turn left and follow the track (Clearwater Lane) to Scaynes Hill. Just across the A272 is **The Farmers.**

6. Return: Walk down Church Road opposite the pub. At Vicarage Lane follow a path parallel to the road over Scaynes Hill Common. Where the road bends right there are two tracks. Take the one on the right and follow it to Yew Tree Cottage. Turn right and follow the edge of a field past a tennis court. Cross a field diagonally

and bear right along the edge of the next. Continue straight across the next field to a private road. Turn left and follow the road round to the right. Just before Pegden take a path on the left through a strip of woodland and cross a field to a corner, by a pole carrying power lines. Bear right along the fence and turn right into a wood. Halfway across an old dam go down to the left along a sunken path. Follow this round to the right and bear left along the edge of the wood with a field on your right. At a junction of paths by a small brick building, turn left and cross a small field. Turn right along a metalled drive, which soon meets a lane (the outward route) by The Sloop. Turn left and follow the lane past Freshfield Mill Farm.

7. Just past Freshmill Cottage turn right over three stiles in rapid succession. Cross a field, aiming for the highest point, and cross the Bluebell Railway to a farm track. Cross a stile on the right, turn left and continue along the edge of a field. Cross a footbridge on the left and bear left over a stile. Turn right uphill, bearing slightly away from the fence, to a signpost on the brow of the hill. Continue to the corner of a hedge and follow it round to the right to a lane. Turn right and just past Town Place cross a stile on the left. Follow the right edges of a large field and a small field and continue through a wood. Continue along the edge of a field to a metalled drive.

8. Turn left and continue to Freshfield Lane. Turn right and just past April Cottage turn left and follow the SBP back to Horsted Keynes.

24. Scaynes Hill to Ditchling

Distance: SBP: 10 km, 6 miles. **Return:** 12 km, 7.5 miles.

Maps: Explorer 135 (18) and 122 (17), Landranger 198.

En route: *Wivelsfield:* pub and shop.

Things to see: *Ditchling:* Museum: local history and arts, summer, Mon-Sat 1030-1700, Sun 1400-1700, winter, weekends only; Church of St Margaret: XIII century; Wings Place: Tudor house, not open to the public.

This walk goes through pleasant countryside, including a lot of woodland in which the paths can be muddy. It is not very hilly, and the best views are of the South Downs, which loom ever larger ahead. The section just north of Ditchling is a maze of paths and small fields and navigation requires care.

---

1. SBP: Take a path (368231) to the right of The Farmers and follow it over two minor roads. Continue along a track and then, at a junction of tracks, along a private road past Ham Lane Farm. Just past Awbrook Park Farm (*not* Awbrook Old Farm), follow the track round to the left. Just before the next house turn right down steps and follow a path round behind the house and into a field. Go downhill along its edge, then across the corner to a stile. Continue along the bottom of the next field and a short way into the next cross a stile into woodland.

2. Cross Ham Bridge, which is just a chunk of concrete, and bear right into Ham Wood. Continue across a track and at a junction of paths bear right along the edge of Strood Wood. Continue along a track to a lane at Moors Cottage (*aka* Slugwash Kennels and Cattery). Turn left along a lane to Wivelsfield.

3. Cross the main road and continue along Eastern Road. The pub shown just to the west on older maps (m/r 345202) no longer exists. Follow the road round to the right and, just before a white cottage (Oak Cottage) on the left, turn left along a track. Continue along a path into West Wood. Just into the wood keep right at a fork. Follow the path through the wood, keeping close to its right-hand edge, and continue past cottages to a road.

4. Turn right, walk to a road junction and cross a footbridge. Turn right along a path and continue along the edge of a field, in the corner of which there are two sets of gates. Cross a stile on the right and follow a grassy track round to the right to a stile on the left. Continue across a large field with scattered trees to a railway bridge (the route along the edge of the field shown on the Explorer map is incorrect). There is a good view to

The Sussex Border Path at Ham Lane, Wilderness Wood, north of Wivelsfield

the South Downs, with the Clayton windmills on the horizon. Over the bridge bear left to a stile in the far corner. Almost at once, cross a stile and footbridge on the right and continue through a strip of woodland. There are two parallel paths at this point; the one on the left boggy and overgrown. The route for the next kilometre is almost a straight line, but care is needed. Continue into the next field and about halfway along cross a stile on the left, which is easily missed. Do not take the stile opposite; turn right and walk between overgrown hedges and across a field. Cross the next field to a gate in a deer fence, where red deer may be seen. Cross a field to another gate which may appear to be padlocked but isn't, and take the right-hand of the next pair of gates. Continue through another gate in the deer fence and over a footbridge. Continue along the right-hand edge of a field, the left-hand edge of the next, and through a strip of woodland.

5. Where the path goes straight on across a footbridge turn right. Continue to the corner of a field, and turn left along a grassy track past Fourfields Farm. Continue a little way into a field to a footbridge and stile on the right. Bear left to cross a field to a stile, just left of its opposite corner. Bear round to the right to a stile in front of a stable block. Bear left by a curving wood fence and follow a path between houses. Continue along a track round to the right to the B2112 and turn left into **Ditchling**.

Ditchling is a popular tourist centre

with artistic connections, and has several art shops and galleries. There are also many old buildings, shops, a tea room, and three pubs: The Sandrock, The Bull and The White Horse.

6. Return: Turn left (east) at the cross-roads and take the second public footpath on the left – Fieldway, a gravelled drive. Continue along a path to East End House and cross to Farm Lane, and very shortly turn left along a path. Cross a small field, bear left over a footbridge and continue along a path into a field. Cross this field and the next, cross a track and go though a gate in a high wire mesh fence (for poultry, not deer), with Fourfields Farm on the left. Bear right across a small field, turn right along the edge of the next, and bear left across the next by a large poultry house, which may not appear on the map. Continue through a small field, cross a footbridge and cross the corner of the next field to a stile about halfway along its edge. Cross the next field to its far corner, with the buildings of Stocks Farm visible on the right. Continue across the corner of the next field and bear left along the edge of the next.

7. Follow the edge of the next field past farm buildings on the left, some of which may not appear on older maps. Continue along the left edge of the next field and through a gate in the deer fence. Go though two similar gates, move left into a field and continue with the deer fence on the right. Go through the final gate in the deer fence and continue along the left edges of two fields. In the next

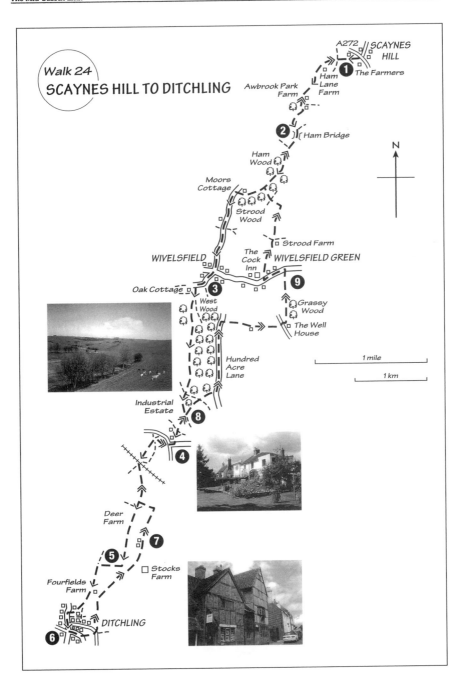

Walk 24

SCAYNES HILL TO DITCHLING

field turn left over a footbridge and continue along the edge of a field and cross two stiles to rejoin the SBP. Turn right and follow the SBP back to the track to West Wood, where there is a sign *Bridleway to Wivelsfield Green*.

8. A little way into the wood a path goes off to the right and, just after this, there is a fork. Keep right where the SBP goes left, and follow the edge of the wood to Hundred Acre Lane. Turn left and follow the lane to a track on the right with a sign *Lashmar*. Follow the track to a road, where the path has been diverted, and may not be as shown on the map. Turn left and just past The Well House take a path on the right. Turn left, follow the path by Grassy Wood to Wivelsfield Green and turn left along the road.

9. Take a road on the right, Strood Gate (if you continue into the village you will come to The Cock Inn and the village stores). Shortly turn right along a private road to Strood Farm and follow it past the farm. At the end of the track continue along a path and across fields to the corner of a wood. Bear left along the edge of a field and enter the wood just past a group of oak trees. Follow a path through the wood to a wide track. Go a little to the left and continue along the path to rejoin the SBP. Turn right and walk back to Scaynes Hill.

Ditchling

25. Ditchling to Patcham

Distance: SBP: 6 km, 3.5 miles. **Return:** 7 km, 4.5 miles. **Patcham:** 2 km, 1 mile.

Maps: Explorer 122 (17), Landranger 198.

Things to see: *Chattri:* Indian war memorial.

This walk may seem short, but it includes two crossings of the main ridge of the South Downs. Save it for a sunny day, for the views are superb. The only blemish is a noisy stretch by the A27.

1. SBP: From the cross-roads in Ditchling (325151) walk south along the B2112 (South Street) to a fork. Take a path between the two roads, signposted *Public Footpath to The Downs*, and follow it to a turning circle. Turn right beside Neville Flats into a field and turn left. Cross a footbridge on the left and bear right across a field towards a road. Follow the right edge of the next field, cross a footbridge and bear right to a gate between two barns. Cross a drive, take a path to the left of stables and follow it through a wood. Cross a field to its far corner, and turn right along Underhill Lane.

2. Take a track on the left signposted *Public Bridleway To Patcham* and follow this round to the right, past a path on the right, and strenuously uphill. At the top, the path meets the South Downs Way. The map may show the SBP going straight across the Way, but this is not correct. Turn right and walk to the Keymer Post. Continue for a few yards to the best viewpoint on the SBP, with views east and west along the ridge of the Downs, south to the sea and north over the Weald to the Surrey hills.

3. Walk a little further to an obvious path on the left (not the right-of-way shown on the map) and follow it across a large field towards the sea. The waymarking along this stretch is for countryside trails rather than the SBP. There are superb views to the west, with Pyecombe and Wolstonbury Hill prominent. Continue across a smaller field. In the next the track swings right past a clump of trees, and Chattri appears on the left. This is a memorial to Indian Hindu and Sikh soldiers who were wounded on the Western Front in the First World War, and who died in the Royal Pavilion (then a War Hospital) in Brighton. They were cremated here, and later the memorial was built.

4. Continue to the next field and, to visit Chattri, walk down to the lower of two gates, where there is a signboard. It is oddly moving to think of these men who died far from home, for a cause of which they knew little or nothing – but how many soldiers in this war really understood what it was about? Continue along the top of the field and the right edge of the next to a minor road above the A27.

The Sussex Border Path south of Ditchling

For the SBP turn right; for the return turn left to a footbridge over the A27.

Patcham: To visit the village cross the footbridge and follow a path round to the right past Horsdean Recreation Ground and uphill along a road. At the top turn left by a house which incorporates a converted oast, and walk down into the old part of **Patcham**, past All Saints Church with its ugly rendering. At the bottom of the hill there is the busy A23 and the Black Lion (hotel, restaurant and pub); opposite is a Youth Hostel. If you turn left along Old London Road, you will find a Tandoori restaurant and a tea room. A little further on there is a small shopping centre. In spite of being surrounded by two busy roads and the modern suburbs of Brighton, Patcham still has the air of a country village, with many attractive old buildings.

5. Return: From the footbridge, go east for a short distance and turn left along a track. Follow this up onto the Downs where it becomes vague. Cross a stile at the corner of a field and continue between barbed wire fences. Continue through a gate along the top of a field. Go under power lines and cross a field, keeping below the crest. Cross the corner of another field to Ditchling Road.

6. Cross the road and follow a path through a wood beside the road. Where the path forks keep left and re-cross the road. Take a path downhill and turn right along a path which runs along the upper edge of a

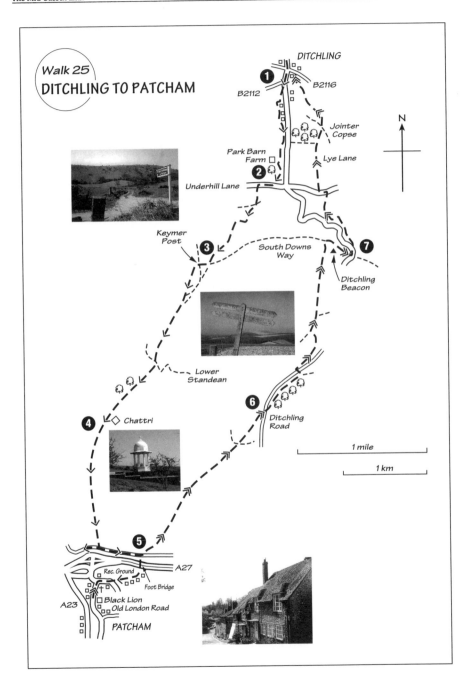

Walk 25
DITCHLING TO PATCHAM

Patcham

bowl-shaped field. At the far corner turn right uphill along a track. Continue past a track on the right, where the zigzag shown on the map hardly exists on the ground. Continue to the South Downs Way and turn right to Ditchling Beacon. The trig point at 814 feet (246 metres) is one of the highest points on the South Downs, and is set almost in the middle of an Iron Age hill fort. Continue to the car park, a popular spot where ice-cream may be had in the summer.

7. Turn left along the road, and shortly take a path on the right. Follow this steeply downhill to a lane. Turn left and shortly right along Lye Lane, a track. Cross a concrete drive and continue along a path past Jointer Copse. Keep left where a path goes off by a small pond. Keep right at a fork, and shortly cross a stile on the left. Continue along the right edge of a field, then bear left to cross three fields diagonally. Take a path between hedges, and bear left and then right along a metal drive back to Ditchling.

26. Patcham to Mile Oak

Distance: SBP: 12 km, 7.5 miles. **Return:** 9 km, 5.5 miles.

Maps: Explorer 122 (17), Landranger 198.

En route: *Devil's Dyke Hotel.*

Things to see: *Saddlescombe:* donkey wheel house: XVII century water pump at Manor Farm. The Devil's Dyke: vast natural hollow. *Portslade:* Church of St Nicholas: XII century; Old Manor: XII century ruins by church, by arrangement with staff at Foredown Tower, tel: 01273 422540; Foredown Tower: camera obscura, weather and astronomy centre, refreshments and toilets, Thu-Sun 1000-1700, tel: 01273 292092.

This walk consists almost entirely of downland, and includes the famous Devil's Dyke. The views are excellent, marred only by numerous pylons and the sprawling coastal towns. Another one to save for a sunny day.

---

1. SBP: Turn right along the minor road above the A27 (302094) and follow it round to the right. Turn left to cross the A23 and the railway by a single footbridge. Turn right along a path beside the railway, then join a track and follow it uphill. This section is shared by the North Brighton Countryside Trail, and is waymarked as such. At a T-junction of tracks turn right and continue uphill for one-and-a-half kilometres, with steadily improving views of the Downs. Where the track swings right and another joins on the left, keep straight on across a field, and then along the lower edge of two more fields. The hamlet of Saddlescombe, pronounced Sa'lscom, appears on the left. At a group of three gates, the path joins the South Downs Way, and the sign-posts and waymarks for the next stretch are for the Way rather than the SBP. Turn slightly left and go downhill to Saddlescombe. Continue along a track past the farm buildings on the left, and turn left down to a road.

2. Cross the road and take a track which leads uphill, by a NT sign *Devil's Dyke.* The steep flanks of the Dyke can be seen on the right. Follow the path uphill and to the right past a reservoir. As you approach the top, bear right to keep just below the road. The Devil's Dyke Hotel appears on the right. At the top of the hill, where the path meets the road, a brief detour towards the hotel gives impressive views down the great hollow of the Dyke. The legend has it that the Devil started to dig the Dyke to let in the sea to drown the

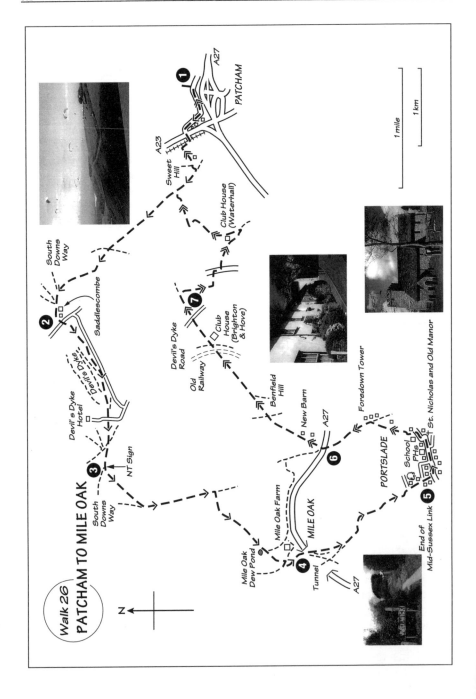

Walk 26
PATCHAM TO MILE OAK

churches of The Weald, but was interrupted when an old lady lit a candle to investigate the noise. Thinking it was dawn, the Devil fled. This being England, another possibility is that somebody's dog got lost down a rabbit-hole. If you are hungry or thirsty you can continue to the hotel. Cross the road and head across a field towards the towers of the radio station on Truleigh Hill. This is a popular area, particularly with hand-gliding enthusiasts. There are fine views to the north and the sea can be seen to the south.

3. At this point the route which may be shown on your map is impassable. Instead of turning left at a junction of several paths, continue to a gate where there is a NT sign *Fulking Escarpment*. Turn half left and follow a faint path SW to a gate near the corner of a field. Through the gate, bear left along the edge of a field. Just after going under power cables, take a track on the right and follow it to the Mile Oak Dew Pond, where there is a wooden plaque with a quotation from Kipling. Just past here, where the track swings left to Mile Oak Farm, take another track on the right going downhill towards a pylon.

4. At the bottom, turn sharp back to the right, pass the pylon and turn left over a stile. Follow a track uphill beside a fence, first to the left and then to the right. The houses of Mile Oak appear on the left. Just before a NT sign *Southwick Hill* take a grassy path on the left and continue with a steep slope on the left. Take your choice between a gate and a stile and continue towards the sea with a tall

hedge on the left. The path turns left under a pylon and then right. Continue between houses on the left and open ground on the right. Cross Mile Oak Gardens and continue along a path beside a pylon. This brings you to Mile Oak Road, a tatty sign *Southwick*, and the rather disappointing end of the Mid-Sussex Link.

5. Return: Turn left and continue into **Portslade** along Mile Oak Road and then High Street, where there are two pubs, the St. George and The Stag's Head. If you turn right along South Street you will find a few shops and a fish bar. Portslade is like Patcham, the old village surviving amidst modern developments. Continue uphill along High Street past some old houses. Where the road swings left a detour along a path on the right will bring you to the Church of St Nicholas and the ruins of Portslade Old Manor. Cross a road by the Old Riding Stables and follow a path uphill past a school. On the right is the Emmaus Shop and Cafe, open Tuesday to Saturday 1000 – 17000, in aid of the homeless. Just past the school turn left along a bridleway and follow it right, left and right again to a road. Cross the road, follow a path to Blackthorn Close and continue along another path, aiming for the Foredown Tower. Cross a road and a field to the Tower, and turn left along a lane.

6. Continue into downland and cross the A27 bridge. Follow a track down to New Barn (Newbarn?) Farm, an equestrian centre, then over Benfield Hill and down into Benfield Valley, aiming for the prominent ╱white

The plaque at Mile Oak Dew Pond, near the end of the Mid-Sussex Link

buildings of the Brighton and Hove Golf Club. Follow a path along the edge of a field beside the golf course. At the top corner of the field the path crosses the course of the old Devil's Dyke Railway, about which there is an informative signboard. Join a track and go past the clubhouse to cross the Devil's Dyke Road.

7. Cross a field, and in the next turn right and follow its edge uphill. At the top turn left by a tall hedge and fence which enclose a gas installation. Turn right along the road, and then left along the drive to Waterhall Golf Course. Walk past the clubhouse and continue downhill for about 150 metres, then turn sharp back left and follow a track which winds downhill along the edge of the golf course. At the bottom of the hill

turn right and cross a field in the bottom of a valley. Continue uphill across the next field, aiming for the left end of a row of small trees. Bear right to a stile and a track and turn right to follow the SBP back to Patcham.

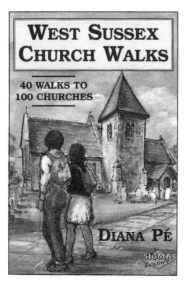

Also of Interest:

WEST SUSSEX CHURCH WALKS

So much more than a walking guide, West Sussex Church Walks contains absorbing histories of the churches featured on each route, plus local history details which enable readers to imagine how people lived in the area up to 1000 years ago. Diana Pe's carefully planned walks range from 3 to 10 miles and cover a variety of terrain from coastal plains and woodland to meandering riversides and gently undulating hills. Fully illustrated with sketch maps and photographs. *£7.95*

A YEAR OF WALKS: SUSSEX

12 circular walks, one for each month of the year, which visit exceptional Sussex locations. You've the option of a full or half-day walk to each spot, whilst the month-by-month approach encourages you to walk in harmony with the seasons. The guide gives you fresh insight into this popular region with its two areas of outstanding beauty - the South Downs and the High Weald.
"All walkers who love a good stroll through the wonderful Sussex countryside will enjoy 'A Year of Walks' "
PORTSMOUTH JOURNAL *£6.95*

BEST TEA SHOP WALKS IN SURREY & SUSSEX

A leisurely walk in the long-neglected countryside of Surrey and Sussex followed by a delicious afternoon tea. "An enjoyable mixture of rambling and relaxation...This book offers a quintessentially English slice of life." SURREY ADVERTISER. *£6.95*

In case of difficulty, or for a free catalogue, please contact:
SIGMA LEISURE, 1 SOUTH OAK LANE, WILMSLOW, CHESHIRE SK9 6AR.
Phone: 01625-531035. Fax: 01625-536800.
E-mail: info@sigmapress..co.uk

Web site: http//www.sigmapress.co.uk

VISA and MASTERCARD welcome